Cultural Atlas for Young People

THE MIDDLE AGES

Mike Corbishley

Facts On File
New York • Oxford

Managing Editor: Lionel Bender
Art Editor: Ben White
Designer: Malcolm Smythe
Text Editor: Miles Litvinoff
Assistant Editor: Madeleine Samuel
Project Editor: Graham Speake
Cartographic Editors: Olive Pearson,
Christine Johnston and Sarah Rhodes
Design Consultant: John Ridgeway
Production: Clive Sparling

Advisory Editor of the series: Gillian Evans,
Fitzwilliam College, Cambridge
Advisory Editor for this volume: Donald Matthew,
University of Reading

AN EQUINOX BOOK

Planned and produced by:
Equinox (Oxford) Ltd,
Musterlin House,
Jordan Hill Road, Oxford,
England OX2 8DP

Prepared by Lionheart Books

Media conversion and typesetting:
Peter MacDonald, Vanessa Hersey
and Una Macnamara

Copyright © Equinox (Oxford) Ltd 1990

Library of Congress Cataloguing-in-Publication
Data

Corbishley, Mike
      The Middle Ages/Mike Corbishley
         p. cm. -- (Cultural atlas for young
         people)
      Includes index.
      Summary: Maps, charts, illustrations, and
text explore the history and culture of the
Middle Ages.
      ISBN 0-8160-1973-8
      1. Civilization, Medieval--Juvenile
literature. [1. Civilization, Medieval. 2. Middle
Ages.]
I. Title II. Series
CB351.S67 1989
940.1--dc19   88-31692

Published in North America by
Facts On File, Inc.,
460 Park Avenue South,
New York, N.Y. 10016

Origination by J. Film Process, Singapore

Second printing

Printed in Italy

Artwork and Picture Credits
All maps drawn by Lovell Johns, Oxford.

Key: t = top, b = bottom, c = center, l = left, r = right etc.
Abbreviations: BM British Museum. CF Chris Forsey. KM
Kevin Maddison.
Title page: Alan Hutchison Library. 5 Dominique Martinez.
6-7 M. Smythe. 10-11 Bridgeman Art Library. 14l KM. 14r
BM. 16 Equinox. 17 Scala, Florence. 18 KM. 18 BM. 19
Scala, Florence. 20t Service de Documentation, Paris. 20bl
Equinox Picture Archive, Oxford. 20br Leonard von Matt,
Buochs. 21 Pierpont Morgan Library, NY. 22t Michael
Holford. 22cl Norfolk Museums Service. 22-23 KM. 24
University Museum of National Antiquities, Oslo. 25 KM. 27l
Bodleian Library, Oxford. 27r British Library, London. 28
Michael Holford. 30 KM. 30-31 Michael Holford, Loughton.
32 KM. 33t Bodleian Library, Oxford. 33b Aerofilms. 34t A.F.
Kersting, London. 34b KM. 36t Universitäts – Bibliothek,
Jena. 36b KM. 38bl Sonia Halliday, Weston Turville. 38br
Master and Fellows of Trinity College, Cambridge. 38-39 KM.
39t CF. 39bl CF. 39br Mike Corbishley. 40t Michel Vuillemin,
Troyes. 40b Robert Harding Picture Library Ltd. 41 Bodleian
Library, Oxford. 42bl Dick Barnard, Milverton. 42br KM.
42-43 Dick Barnard, Milverton. 44,45 Sonia Halliday, Weston
Turville. 46t Historik Museum, Bergen. 46b Michael Dixon,
Dover. 47t Master and Fellows of Magdalene College,
Cambridge. 47bl Kunsthistorisches Museum, Vienna. 47br
Christopher Page, Oxford. 48t Ronald Sheridan. 48b History
of Science Museum, Oxford. 49tl Österreichische
Nationalbibliothek, Vienna. 49tr British Library, London. 49bl
Mary Evans Picture Library, London. 49br Bibliothèque
Nationale, Paris. 50-51 Bridgeman Art Library. 52t Michael
Holford, Loughton. 52b Victoria and Albert Museum, London.
42-53 Bibliothèque Nationale, Paris. 53t Graham Speake,
Oxford. 54t Bodleian Library, Oxford. 54b, 58 Bibliothèque
Nationale, Paris. 58-59 KM. 60 Biblioteca Apostolica
Vaticana. 62t Robert Harding Associates, London. 62bl, 62br
Michael Dixon, Dover. 63cr Leonard von Matt, Buochs. 63bl
Michael Holford, Loughton. 65l Franco Ragazzi, Bologna. 65r
British Library, London. 66t Edwin Smith, Saffron Walden.
66b Robert Harding Picture Library, London. 68t Alan
Hutchison Library, London. 68c Dick Barnard, Milverton. 68b
Zefa, London. 69 CF. 70t Biblioteca Apostolica Vaticana.
70bl, br Bibliothèque Nationale, Paris. 71 Musée Condé,
Chantilly. 72 Michael Holford, Loughton. 73 Sonia Halliday,
Weston Turville. 74l University Library, Ghent. 74r Public
Record Office, London. 75 KM. 76tr Andrew Lawson, Oxford.
76cr Leonard von Matt, Buochs. 76bl Graham Speake,
Oxford. 77 John Fuller, Cambridge. 78t Zefa, London. 78c
Dorian Gerhold, London. 78b Dr L. Beckel, Bad Ischl, Austria.
80 Fairford, Glos. 80-81 KM. 81t,b Sonia Halliday, Weston
Turville. 82t Michael Dixon, Dover. 82b Ekdotike Athenon,
S.A., Athens. 84bl Giraudon, Paris. 84br Tretyakov Gallery,
Moscow. 86-87 KM. 88, 90 Werner Forman Archive. 91 KM.

Quote from *The Canterbury Tales* by Geoffrey Chaucer taken
from translation by Nevill Coghill (Penguin Classics, Revised
Edition 1977), Copyright 1951 by Nevill Coghill, copyright ©
Nevill Coghill, 1958,1960,1975,1977.

CONTENTS

Introduction 4
Table of Dates 6

Europe · Physical 8

PART ONE:
A HISTORY OF MEDIEVAL EUROPE
Europe AD 350 to 1500 12
The Barbarian Movements 14
The Empire of Justinian 16
Ravenna 18
Carolingian Europe 20
Sutton Hoo 22
Viking Expansion 24
The Byzantine Empire 26
The Plantagenet Empire 28
The Bayeux Tapestry 30
Domesday Book 32
The Crusades 34
The German Empire 36
The Medieval Church 38
Education 40
Cathedral Building 42
Stories in Stained Glass 44
Medieval Arts and Crafts 46
Science, Medicine and Printing 48

PART TWO:
THE LANDS OF MEDIEVAL EUROPE
Travel 52
France 54
Medieval Paris 58
Italy 60
Italy · Sites 62
Trade 64
The British Isles 66
Castles 68
The Countryside 70
Spain and Portugal 72
Mapmaking 74
Journey to Compostela 76
Switzerland, Germany and the
    Low Countries 78
Everyday Life 80
Bohemia, Hungary, Greece
    and the Balkans 82
Lithuania, Poland and Russia 84
A Russian Village 86
Scandinavia 88
Scandinavia · Sites 90

Glossary & Further Reading 92
Gazetteer 93
Index 95

INTRODUCTION

This is a book about the peoples of medieval Europe. But what does the word "medieval" mean? It comes from two Latin words meaning "middle age." In fact many writers still call this period of history the middle ages, hence the title of our book. What were they in the middle of? The medieval age begins at the end of the Roman period in western Europe, about AD350. It ends with the discovery, by Europeans, of the world beyond Europe in the late 15th century.

We started by talking about "peoples" of medieval Europe. In this book you will read about a number of different peoples over a period that covers more than one thousand years. Some of these peoples were relatively small in number but have had great influence on later periods. The Vikings were such a people. No huge armies of Vikings sailed from their homelands of Scandinavia but their influence can still be seen today in towns and settlements across northern Europe and beyond to Iceland, Greenland and even North America.

Because there were a number of peoples looking for new lands or just eager for power, the boundaries between countries frequently changed. Here you will be able to read about, and follow on the maps, at least part of the story of each "country" in medieval Europe. Some of these became "world powers," as we say today. Part of the story of medieval Europe is the struggle between these world powers. For example, there were wars between Christians and the followers of the prophet Muhammad, whose religion is Islam – the Muslim peoples. You will probably already have read about the Crusades to win back the Holy Land (Palestine), but there were other struggles going on. There was also a conflict between different types of Christian worship.

How do we discover the evidence for the peoples of medieval Europe? As for all historic periods there are two main sources. Documents give us one form of evidence that can be read. Archaeological evidence is the physical remains of the past – perhaps a leather shoe preserved in a well, or a great cathedral still in use today. These two very different types of evidence together help build up the picture we have of the past.

The book is divided into two main sections. The first, **A History of Medieval Europe**, looks at the development of the most important empires that set the boundaries in the past. The second section, **The Lands of Medieval Europe**, examines in greater detail the individual countries that we can all recognize today and their own histories.

The Middle Ages is an atlas so there are lots of maps to help you understand the development of Europe. As you read through the book, compare the various regions with the map of Europe today on pages 8 and 9 to see how different medieval Europe really was – the past is a foreign country! But there is much more to this book than just maps. In both sections you will find a number of special features that look at life in medieval times and at some of the remains that you can see today. Our story is arranged in double-page spreads, so you can read the book from beginning to end, or just dip into it to learn about a specific topic. The Glossary on page 92 contains definitions of historical terms used in the book.

Abbreviations used in this book
AD = Anno Domini (the year of the Lord; of the Christian era).
BC = Before Christ. c. = circa (about). in = inch. ft = foot. mi = mile.

▷ The town of Cordes (Tarn), founded in 1222.

TABLE OF DATES

	300	400	500	600	700	800
ARTS AND ARCHITECTURE		Christian Churches built in Rome, Jerusalem, Constantinople	532-37 St Sophia, Constantinople c.550 Ravenna mosaics	c.650 Sutton Hoo ship burial c.698 Lindisfarne Gospels	735-804 Alcuin, scholar	c.870 *Codex Aure* illustrated manuscript

Diocletian and Maximian, c.300.

St Sophia, Constantinople, 532-37.

The emperor Charlemagne, crowned 800.

	300	400	500	600	700	800
CHRISTIAN CHURCH	313 Edict of Milan granting toleration to Christians	430 death of Augustine at Hippo Regius 451 Council of Chaceldon	526 death of St Benedict 560-Irish missions to Continent 590-604 Gregory I pope			817 Benedict of Aniane reforms monasteries 860 Cyril and Methodius sent to Moravia
ROMAN EMPIRE	395 divison of the Empire		533 Africa restored to Roman Empire	610-41 Heraclius emperor	716-17 Muslim siege of Constantinople 717-41 Leo III emperor 730-843 iconoclasm	867-86 Basil I, first emperor of Macedonian dynasty
ISLAM				622 Muhammad goes to Medina 661-80 Muawiya, first Umayyad caliph at Damascus	762 foundation of Baghdad as Abbasid capital	909 foundation of Fatimid caliphate in N. Africa
SPAIN		409 Vandals, Alans and Suevi enter Spain	509 Visigoths defeated at Vouillé and fall back on Spain		711 Muslims invade Spain	c.860 serious Viking assaults on Spain
FRANCE		486 Clovis defeats Syagrius	c.507 conversion of Clovis to Catholicism	687 Pepin of Austrasia defeats Neustrians at Tertry	732 Charles Martel defeats Saracens at Poitiers 751 Pepin III becomes king of the Franks	888 Odo count of Paris becomes king
ITALY		476 Odovacar king of Italy	536 Belisarius reconquers Rome 568 Lombard invasion of Italy	668 Constans II killed at Syracuse	774 Charlemagne becomes king of Italy	
GERMANY		406 Germans cross the Rhine			772-804 Saxon wars	800 Charlemagne crowned emperor 843 Treaty of Verdun: empire divided
EASTERN EUROPE	341 Ulfila begins conversion of Goths 376 Goths cross the Danube		Slavs begin to infiltrate Balkans			864 conversion of Bulgars
BRITAIN AND IRELAND			563 St Columba in Iona 597 Roman mission to England	664 Synod of Whitby	Mercian supremacy 731 Bede completes *Ecclesiastical History* 793 first Viking raids on England	836 Danes established at Dublin 899 death of Alfred Wessex kings of England
SCANDINAVIA						860 Danes established in Iceland

6

900	1000	1100	1200	1300	1400	1500
c.985 *Beowulf*	c.1063 San Marco, Venice	1194-1220 Chartres cathedral built	c.1225-74 Aquinas 1265-1321 Dante 1266-1337 Giotto	1304-74 Petrarch 1345-1400 Chaucer 1377-1446 Brunelleschi 1386-1466 Donatello c.1390-1441 van Eyck	c.1400-74 Dufay 1452-1519 Leonardo da Vinci 1471-1528 Dürer	

Viking ship, Oseberg, h century

The Tower of London, c.1080.

Sculptures from Chartres cathedral, 1134-50.

The town hall, Siena, 1297-1376.

David by Donatello, 1430.

900	1000	1100	1200	1300	1400	1500
911 foundation of Cluny	1046 Synod of Sutri – beginning of reform in Roman church	1115 foundation of Clairvaux 1179 Lateran Council III	1209 Franciscan order approved 1215 Paris university receives first statutes	c1309-77 Pope's residence at Avignon 1378 schism begins	1415-17 Council of Constance	
963-69 Nicephorus Phocas emperor	1018 final defeat of Bulgars 1071 battle of Manzikert	1176 Manuel I defeated by Seljuksat Myriokephalon	1204 4th crusade; capture of Constantinople 1261 restoration of empire		1453 capture of Constantinople	
	1055 Seljuks capture Baghdad 1071 after Manzikert Seljuks occupy Asia Minor 1095 1st Crusade	1171 Saladin conquers Fatimid Egypt 1187 Saladin recaptures Jerusalem	1218-21 5th Crusade 1250-1517 Mamluk dynasty in Egypt 1291 last Latin states in Holy Land taken by Mamluks	1326 Ottomans take Bursa 1389 Ottomans defeat Serbs at Kosovo	1402 death of Timur the Lame 1453 Muslims capture Constantinople	
929 Umayyad caliphate in Spain	1031 end of Cordoban caliphate 1085 Christians capture Toledo	1137 count of Barcelona becomes king of Aragon 1147 Lisbon captured from Muslims	1235-48 Catholics conquer Cordoba and Seville	1369 Trastamara dynasty in Castile	1479 Ferdinand V of Aragagon marries Isabella of Castile 1492 discovery of "New World" 1498 Vasco da Gama reaches India	
911 Rollo installed in Normandy 987 Hugh, first Capetian king of the Franks			1204 Philip II conquers lands in France 1210-29 Albigensian wars 1226-70 Louis IX 1284 war between England and France	1337 war begins between Philip VI of Valois and Edward III	1431 Joan of Arc burned 1477 death of Charles the Rash, last Valois duke of Burgundy	
962 Otto I crowned emperor	1030 Normans established at Aversa	1130-54 Roger II king of Sicily	1212-50 Frederick II emperor and king of Sicily 1252 first florins struck in Florence	1347 plague reaches Genoa from Crimea 1385 Gian Galeazzo unites Visconti lands	1434 Cosimo de Medici returns to Florence 1454 Peace of Lodi	
955 Otto I defeats Magyars at the Lech		1122 Concordat of Worms 1159-77 imperial-papal quarrel	1273 Rudolf of Hapsburg elected king of the Romans 1291 first Swiss alliance	1338 Declaration of Rense 1348 university founded at Prague	1419-36 Hussite wars	
966 foundation of Poland 989 Vladimir of Kiev becomes Christian	1000 Otto III founds archdiocese at Gniezno 1001 kingdom of Hungary established		1241 Mongols defeat Christians at Legnica	1320 Polish kingdom reunited 1386 Poland ruled with Lithuania	1478 Ivan III takes Novgorod	
973 first recorded coronation of an English king	1017 Canute becomes king of England 1066 Norman conquest of England 1086 Domesday Book	1154 Henry II first Angevin king of England	1215 Magna Carta 1284 English king establishes rule over Wales 1296 war with Scotland	1381 peasants' revolt	1483 Henry Tudor made king	
995-c.1000 Olaf I king of Norway		1104 archbishopric of Lund founded		1397 Norway, Sweden and Denmark united by Kalmar Union		

EUROPE · PHYSICAL

What do you understand by the word "Europe"? Perhaps it will depend where you live – whether your home is in Europe or in one of the other six continents, the great land masses that make up our world. For you Europe might be a place you go to for a vacation or a place where you can see and wonder at the great monuments of the past.

Europe today

There are several ways of defining Europe today. The European Community (EC) began with six countries in 1958. The countries were Belgium, France, West Germany, Italy, Luxembourg and the Netherlands. Today there are twelve countries in the Community, including the United Kingdom, Spain and Greece.

Another way of thinking about Europe is to include both western European countries (west as far as Ireland and Portugal) and eastern European countries (east as far as the Soviet Union and Greece).

The physical shape of Europe

Yet another way of defining Europe is to look at the physical boundaries, especially those between the continents of Europe and Asia. These boundaries are the mountain ranges of the Caucasus (between the Black Sea and the Caspian Sea) and the Urals (in the Soviet Union), both just off our map to the east.

Medieval Europe

The definition of Europe we use in this book about the medieval period is quite different. It has to be. We must start with what the Romans thought of as their Empire – and add to it as necessary. We must add countries and areas at different times in the medieval period. To the question "What exactly is Europe?" a Roman would not have been able to give a reply. An educated person from medieval Europe would have known what the question meant and been able to respond.

▷ This map shows you the modern boundaries of the Europe you are going to read about in this book. You will see that these boundaries are often quite different from those in the medieval period. The physical features are important. Mountain ranges, seas, deserts and rivers usually defined where people lived and where they could travel to.

8

C   D   E   F   L Ladoga   4   G

NORWAY   **FINLAND**
                                              ■ Helsinki   Rybuisk   Volga
  ■ Oslo   Reservoir
     ■ Stockholm   L Peipus   Oka
  L Vanern   ■ Moscow   3
     L Vattern
  SWEDEN   Dvina
                                                                                        CENTRAL
                        Gotland   **RUSSIAN**
DENMARK   Baltic Sea   **UPLANDS**
     ■ Copenhagen   Neman   Dnieper
        Bornholm   **UNION OF SOVIET SOCIALIST REPUBLICS**

                                                        NORTH EUROPEAN PLAIN   Don
Weser   Elbe **EAST**   Vistula   Pripet
                                                          Marshes   Pripet
      Berlin ■   ■ Warsaw
  GERMANY   Oder **POLAND**   Dnieper

                                                                                                                          Don
             ■ Prague   Dniester   2
  WEST   **CZECHOSLOVAKIA**   Prut
  GERMANY   **CARPATHIAN MTS**   Sea of Azov
BLACK Danube   2
FOREST   Vienna ■   Tisza   **ROMANIA**
  L Constance   ■ Budapest
LIECHTENSTEIN   **AUSTRIA**   L Balaton   **TRANSYLVANIAN ALPS**
WITZERLAND   Drava   **HUNGARY**   Black Sea
PS   **DOLOMITES**
  Po   ■ Belgrade   ■ Bucharest
SAN   **DINARIC ALPS**   Danube
MARINO ○   **YUGOSLAVIA**   **BULGARIA**
                                           Drina   **PONTINE MTS**
  APENNINES   ■ Sofia   **BALKAN MTS**
  Tiber ■ Rome   Adriatic Sea   Axios   △ Musala
                                                             9590   ■ Ankara
Corsica   **ITALY**   ■ Tiranë   Kizil Irmak   △ Demirkazik
                                     ALBANIA   12820
Sardinia   △ Mt Olympos   **TURKEY**   L Tuz
                                     PINDUS 9564   Aegean   L Beysehir   1
  Tyrrhenian Sea   Ionian   **MTS**   Sea   **TAURUS MTS**
                       Sea   **GREECE**
                                              ■ Athens   Menderes
         Sicily   △ Mt Etna   **SYRIA**
                    10895   Rhodes
  ■ Tunis   **CYPRUS** ■ Nicosia   **LEBANON**
                                                                                                                      ■ Beirut
TUNISIA   **MALTA**   Crete

           Mediterranean Sea   **ISRAEL**

PART ONE

A HISTORY OF MEDIEVAL EUROPE

△ A 10th-century ivory book cover showing Pope Gregory the Great at his writing desk.

▷ Detail from an early medieval illuminated manuscript, the Lindisfarne Gospels. Lindisfarne Island, off the northeast coast of England, was a focal point of English Christianity from 635 to about 950.

Europe AD 350 to 1500

Roman Empire
Diocletianic diocese boundary
East-west division of Empire, 395
Territorial boundary
• Important settlement

Scale 1 : 24 000 000

0 ——— 600 km
0 ——— 400 miles

North Sea

Baltic Sea

BRITAIN
• Londinium

ATLANTIC OCEAN

• Colonia Agrippina
Rhine
Lutetia • GAUL
Loire
• Caesarodunum
Burdigala • Lugdunum
VIENNENSIS • Vienna
WEST ROMAN EMPIRE

PANNÓNIA
• Aquileia
Danube
• Sirmium
• Ravenna

Black Sea

SPAIN
Tagus
• Toletum
• Emerita Augusta
Narbonne •
Corsica
ITALY
• Rome
MOESIA
THRACE
• Constantinople
• Thessalonica
• Ancyra • PONTUS
• Amida

Sardinia

Balearic Is
• Carthago Nova
Sicily
EAST ROMAN EMPIRE
• Smyrna
ASIA
• Athens
• Antioch

• Carthage
Cyprus *Crete* ORIENS

AFRICA
Mediterranean Sea
• Jerusalem

◁ Europe in 350. For centuries the Romans had increased the size of the lands they controlled. At its biggest there were probably as many as 60 million people living in the Roman Empire. It was always difficult to control parts of this great Empire, especially those provinces that were on the borders. The problem was ruling such a huge area. Diocletian (made Roman Emperor in 284) split the huge Empire into two. He ruled from the East and appointed Maximian to rule in the West. To help organize and control this Empire, he divided it into 12 dioceses – marked here on the map. After the Emperor Theodosius' death in 395 the Empire was ruled separately in East and West.

Frankish Empire
Frontier land (march)
East Roman Empire
Muslim land
Territorial boundary
Picts Name of people
• Important settlement

Scale 1 : 24 000 000

0 ——— 600 km
0 ——— 400 miles

Scots **Picts**
North Sea
NORTHUMBRIA
Danes
Baltic Sea

Welsh
MERCIA
WESSEX • London

ATLANTIC OCEAN

• Cologne
Rhine
• Paris
• Metz
• Regensburg
Danube
FRANKISH EMPIRE
PANNONIA
• Poitiers
• Lyon
• Venice
Slavs
BULGAR KHANATE
• Milan
• Ravenna
• Belgrade

• Oviedo
GALICIA
SPANISH MARCH
PAPAL STATE
Corsica
Narbonne •
DUCHY OF BENEVENTO
• Durazzo
• Thessalonica
Black Sea
• Trebizond
• Constantinople

Tagus
• Toledo
• Barcelona
• Rome
• Benevento
• Ancyra
UMAYYAD EMIRATE
Lisbon •
• Valencia
Sardinia
EAST ROMAN EMPIRE
• Almería
Balearic Is
Sicily
• Smyrna
• Tangier
• Athens
• Antioch

IDRISID CALIPHATE
AGHLABID EMIRATE
Mediterranean Sea
Cyprus *Crete*
ABBASID CALIPHATE
• Jerusalem

◁ Europe in 800. By the year 800 the West Empire had broken down and several "barbarian" states had been founded. The Romans called those who lived beyond their boundaries, who did not speak their Latin language or live the Roman way of life, *barbari* – our word "barbarians." The East Roman (Byzantine) Empire based in Constantinople still kept its influence in the East, in southern Italy and Sardinia. Other parts of the old Empire in the West were ruled by the Franks and by the Muslims – followers of the religion of Islam – who dominated north Africa and the Mediterranean Sea. The Frankish Empire under Charlemagne, which was Christian, tried to revive Roman traditions. But by Roman standards even the Franks were barbarians.

▷ Europe in 1150. By the 12th century Roman provinces that the Muslims had gained from the East Roman Empire were won back. Crusading Christians from the West had established Crusader states in the Holy Land, though they were under threat from the Muslims. In the West, Christians had recovered parts of southern Spain and Italy. The Holy Roman (or German) Empire created by the Franks had strengthened its hold on Germany and Italy and had begun to expand eastwards into the territory of the Slavs. At this time it looked as if a new Christian empire would expand to control as large an area as the Romans had once conquered.

▷ Europe in 1500. By 1500 great changes had occurred in Europe. Any hope that a Christian empire might be established throughout the Mediterranean was crushed by the success of a new empire – that of the Ottomans. The East Roman Empire had been overrun by Ottoman Turks. Constantinople itself was captured in 1453. The eastern Empire could no longer be called Christian. The Holy Land, once protected by Western Christians, passed into the hands of the Muslims. A different story was emerging in the West. Several smaller kingdoms were established and powerful rulers fought with each other for control of territories. Nations were being created, often out of a number of different peoples.

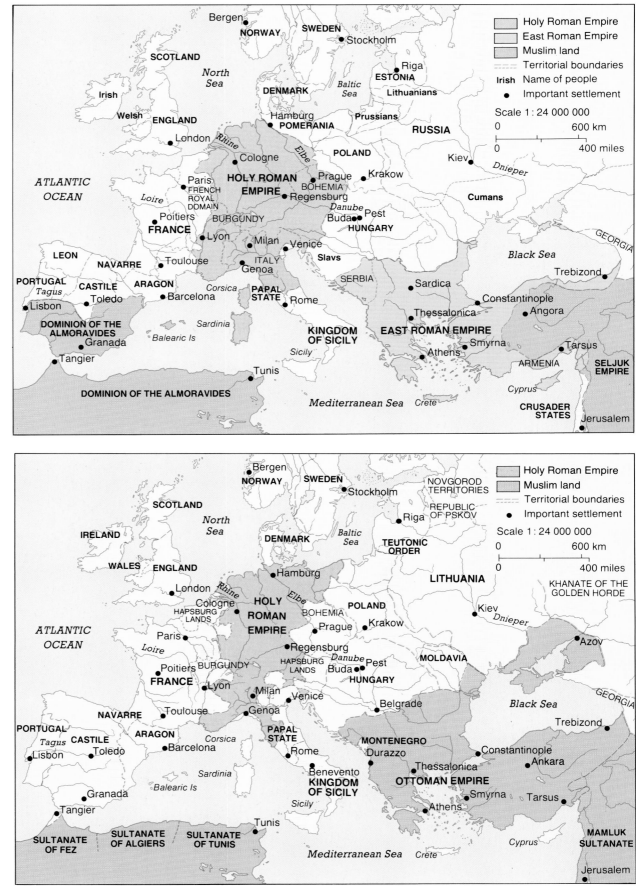

THE BARBARIAN MOVEMENTS

The army of the Visigoths led by Athaulph marched on Gaul... The Romans were no longer able to win back Britain – from now on it continued to be ruled by whoever had seized power.

The year being described is 411. The writer is Procopius, a civil servant who was born about 500 and wrote, among other works, histories of the wars of the Roman Emperor Justinian. We have seen (page 12) that the Romans, in their vast Empire, had suffered from those peoples they called "barbarians." Not all these enemies were uneducated and murderous; they often wanted to rule their own countries and break away from Rome.

From the northwest

From the countries to the north of the River Rhine tribes called Saxons, Angles and Jutes invaded southern Britain. At first they settled alongside Romano-British communities in the eastern part of the country. Like many other barbarians, some were signed up as paid "mercenary" soldiers. Britain was unsettled, though, and many people fled to other parts of the country. Hoards of coins and valuables they hid have been discovered.

Terror from the east

A report spread that the Goths had suddenly descended like a whirlwind from the high mountains and were ravaging and destroying everything in their path.

The historian Ammianus Marcellinus, writing in the 4th century, summed up the Romans' fear of the hordes of invaders. The Goths came from the steppes of Russia. There were two groups – Visigoths and Ostrogoths. Roman emperors paid some of them to stay out of Roman territory or persuaded some to move further west (to Italy and into Gaul). Despite this they

∇ Unsettled conditions in eastern Britain meant that many people chose to bury their wealth for safe-keeping. The scene below depicts the burial of the so-called Thetford treasure. This was a hoard of 4th-century gold and silver objects, probably buried by a merchant, from Thetford in Norfolk. It was discovered by chance in 1979 and is now in the British Museum, London.

△ This gold buckle, from the Thetford treasure, has a hinged bow in the form of two facing horses' heads. The high quality of the metalworking and the style of the figure suggest that it was made on the Continent in the late 4th century.

North Sea

Picts

Jutes

Angles

Saxons

Angles
Saxons
London
Jutes

Franks

Rhine

ARMORICA

WEST ROMAN EMPIRE
Paris

Orléans

Catalaunian Plains

Worms

Alamans

Danube

KINGDOM OF ODOVACAR

Ostrogoths

Vandals, Suevi

Huns

Ostrogoths

ATLANTIC OCEAN

Loire

Burgundians
Lyon

Milan

Verona

Drava

Gepids

Visigoths

Garonne

Po

Ravenna

WEST ROMAN EMPIRE

EAST ROMAN EMPIRE

Suevi

Basques

Toulouse

Narbonne

WEST ROMAN EMPIRE

Plovdiv

VISIGOTHIC KINGDOM

Ebro

Barcelona

Corsica

Rome

Tagus

Toledo

Sardinia

Balearic Islands

Cosenza

Reggio

Athens
Corinth
Sparta

Barbarian movements
→ Franks
→ Huns
→ Ostrogoths
→ Saxons, Angles, Jutes
→ Vandals, Suevi
→ Visigoths

Marsala

Sicily

Crete

VANDAL KINGDOM

Carthage

Mediterranean Sea

– – – Territorial boundary c.475
Angles Name of people
✕ Major battle

Scale 1 : 16 000 000

0   400 km
0   300 miles

△ Migrations of barbarians in the 4th and 5th centuries. There were many reasons for the movement of peoples from outside the Roman world and inside its boundaries. Some were looking for new farmland, but others enjoyed warfare.

Saxons and others

By mid-5th century Saxons, Angles and Jutes have begun to settle in Britain permanently.
410 In Italy, Rome taken by Visigoth chief Alaric.
493 Ravenna falls to Theodoric, king of the Ostrogoths. Theodoric dies fighting with the Romans against the Huns in 526.
West Roman Empire: 414 Visigoths take over Narbonne but abandon the town in 415.
436 Burgundians defeated by Huns at Worms.
451 Attila the Hun defeated by Roman general Aetius with help from barbarian troops at Catalaunian Plains. **486** Franks take over territory in West Roman Empire.
East Roman Empire: 382 Emperor Theodosius allows Visigoths to settle on the northern edge of the Empire. **468** Failure of Emperor Leo's expedition against Vandals.

were unstoppable, taking over huge areas that had once been Roman. Rome was itself plundered by the Visigoths in 410.

Barbarians were human too…

Despite their reputation, the barbarians had their good side. It is true that they did not live a Roman way of life and hardly left any written record of themselves, but some, like the Goths, were Christians, and their skilled metal-workers and jewelers produced magnificent crowns, crosses and elaborate bookcovers. They liked to wear jewelry on their clothes.

15

THE EMPIRE OF JUSTINIAN

The Roman Empire in the East continued to be ruled by emperors at the end the 5th century. But the situation in the West Empire was quite different. There, army commanders usually appointed emperors. In 476 Ordovacar, king of a group of German tribes who had settled in Italy, decided to rule instead of the Emperor Romulus Augustulus.

Reoccupying the West

It was not until the reign of Justinian as Emperor in the East that the West Empire was brought under Roman control again. After he came to power in 527, Justinian's first move against the barbarians who had taken over the Empire was in north Africa. Vandals, originally from central Europe, had swept westwards, through Spain and into Africa early in the 5th century. Although the Vandals had set up a strong kingdom there, Justinian's campaign won back north Africa in a few months in 533.

Generals Belisarius and Narses

The Emperor's two commanders attacked Italy from different directions. Belisarius occupied Sicily, Sardinia and Corsica, and then moved into mainland Italy, finally reoccupying Rome in 536. After a century of fear, Rome was now freed from Vandal power in the Mediterranean.

Narses moved across land to lay siege to Ravenna in 540. Ravenna had become the official residence of the barbarian rulers of Italy – the Ostrogoth Theodoric, for example. There was some resistance to the reoccupation by Roman forces, but this was finally crushed in 552. Narses ruled the West, which now included a small part of Spain, from Ravenna as the Emperor Justinian's chosen governor.

◁ This portrait of the Emperor Justinian is a small part of a large mosaic picture in the church of San Vitale, Ravenna, Italy. The building was begun by the king of the Ostrogoths, Theodoric, in about 520. Justinian had the church decorated with wall and ceiling mosaics in about 550.

▷ The reconquests of Justinian. Compare this map of the countries around the Mediterranean with the one on the previous page. For a short period, at least, Roman authority was reestablished in the West by Justinian. Roman trade could now begin again across the Mediterranean.

– – Territorial boundary
Slavs Name of people
▨ Empire of Justinian, 527
☐ Justinian's reconquests by 565
▨ Disputed land
→ Route of Justinian's campaigns
✕ Major battle
◆ City fortified by Justinian
● Other settlement

Scale 1 : 16 000 000

0 — 300 km
0 — 200 miles

After Justinian

Justinian died in 565. Italy was invaded by the Lombards in 568, but they were not able to take over the whole country. Only in the late 7th century were Africa and then Spain taken over by the Muslims. The East Roman Empire, also known as the Byzantine Empire, continued to be ruled by emperors until 1453 when its capital, Constantinople, fell to the Ottoman Turks.

Events of Justinian's reign

527 Justinian proclaimed Emperor with his wife Theodora.
533 Campaigns against barbarians in Africa and Italy.
535-54 Ostrogoths conquered in Italy.
552 Reoccupation of southern Spain.
Attacks from outside Empire: Slavs **534, 547, 549, 551.** Bulgars **534, 538.** Huns **539-40, 559.** Persian Emperor Khusrau I makes frequent attacks until peace treaty in **561.**
565 Emperor Justinian dies.

△ Part of the helmet of Agilulf, who was King of the Lombards 590-615. Even though the Lombards invaded Italy after Justinian's time, the decoration here shows Agilulf (center with the pointed beard) guarded by his warriors wearing Roman armor.

RAVENNA

Ravenna, a port in northeastern Italy, was enlarged in AD 23 by the first Roman Emperor, Augustus, who based his northern navy there. The city became much more important from 402 when it was chosen as the official residence of the Roman Emperors of the West so that they could have close links with the Emperors in the East in Constantinople.

Imperial buildings

Buildings in Ravenna had to be splendid enough for the court of the Roman Emperor. One that survives today, and influenced later buildings, was the church of Sacra Croce (the Sacred Cross). It was built in about 425 by the Empress Galla Placidia, who was the mother of the Emperor Valentinian III.

Attached to the church was a mausoleum (a building for burial) with beautiful mosaics on its domed ceiling. They show a deep sparkling blue heaven with gold stars shining through.

Christian conquerors

In 493 Ravenna was captured by the Ostrogoth King Theodoric. He governed Italy from here with the help of Roman advisers. He had lived from the age of 8 to 18 in the imperial court at Constantinople. He was, therefore, a well-educated man. During his 30-year reign in Ravenna he put up a number of fine buildings and adapted or changed others. Many of these buildings were Christian churches.

Regained by Justinian

The Roman Emperor in the East, Justinian, sent his forces to drive out the Goths from Italy. After Theodoric's death in 526 Ravenna remained an important city. Justinian had new buildings put up and others adapted – as he did elsewhere in the Empire.

In Ravenna the most important building was the church of San Vitale. The church was begun by the Ostrogothic Bishop of Ravenna but completed by Justinian. It was the official church of the imperial court, built of long thin bricks but with marble columns inside and decorated with splendid mosaics on its upper walls and domed ceilings. One mosaic is a picture of Justinian and Theodora bringing gifts to the holy altar.

▷ This beautiful mosaic dome was commissioned by King Theodoric in Ravenna. It shows Christ being baptized in the River Jordan by John the Baptist (on Christ's left). If you follow around the dome you will see (above Christ's head) a cross on a cushion. You will need to look at the mosaic closely or with a magnifying glass to see the little pieces of stone that make up the picture.

▽ Mosaics – pictures and patterns mainly in stone – were made by both Greek and Roman artists. Rich Romans, especially in southern Italy in places such as Pompeii, used Greek mosaic makers to construct fine floor and wall pictures. The tradition continued in the East Roman Empire.

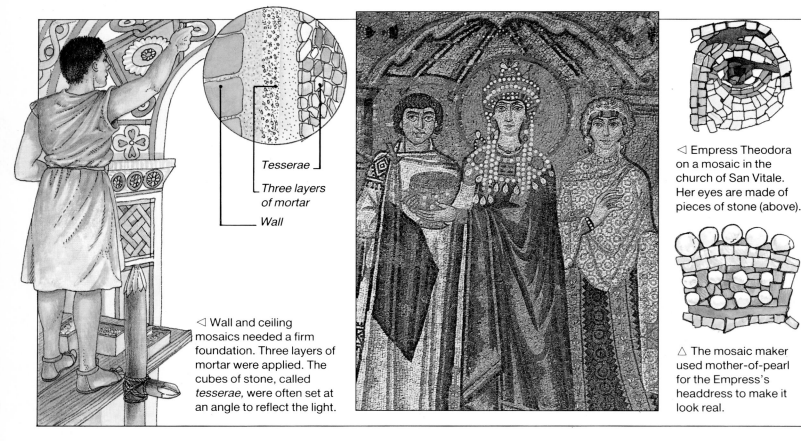

Tesserae

Three layers of mortar

Wall

◁ Wall and ceiling mosaics needed a firm foundation. Three layers of mortar were applied. The cubes of stone, called *tesserae*, were often set at an angle to reflect the light.

◁ Empress Theodora on a mosaic in the church of San Vitale. Her eyes are made of pieces of stone (above).

△ The mosaic maker used mother-of-pearl for the Empress's headdress to make it look real.

CAROLINGIAN EUROPE

Western Europe in the 6th century
When Ostrogoths ruled Italy and Visigoths ruled Spain, the countries we now know as France, Switzerland, Germany, Luxembourg, Belgium and the Netherlands were ruled by a number of different Christian kings. The most powerful rulers were the Franks. They were right on the edge of the Christian world and fought against non-Christian peoples beyond (the Frisians and Saxons). They also established many monasteries in their lands.

The Frankish kingdom of Clovis was later divided into three parts: Austrasia, Neustria and Burgundy. One of these kingdoms, Austrasia (now Germany), became powerful not only because its people were warlike but also because they controlled the main route between the newly established Christian communities in England and Rome itself. Pilgrims and monks had to go through Austrasia and across the Alps into Italy, as the route through southern Gaul (now France) was blocked by the Saracen Muslims.

The Carolingian family
Charles Martel was the first of the Carolingian family to have a reputation in Europe – his name means Charles the Hammer. He defeated the Saracen Muslims at Poitiers (in western France) in 732. He made himself the most powerful ruler in the whole of Gaul. His son, Pepin III, won back lost territories and conquered new lands. He was the first of the family to become king of all the Franks.

By Pepin III's death in 768, the Frankish empire stretched from the borders of Spain to the Netherlands, and east from the edge of Brittany to Bohemia.

Charles the Great – Charlemagne
Pepin's two sons inherited his lands. When the younger son died in 771, the elder, Charles, became sole ruler. This Charles was called, in Latin, Carolus Magnus, or Charles the Great – Charlemagne. The word Carolingian comes from his name Carolus. Charlemagne reigned as emperor for over 45 years and increased the size of the empire. He organized about 60 military campaigns – leading half of them himself. His wars against the Saxons were long, drawn-out and brutal.

By the end of the 8th century the boundaries of the Carolingian Empire had moved north to take over the Saxon lands, south into Italy and east into Bavaria. The pope in Rome recognized Charlemagne's considerable authority and crowned him Emperor of the West.

Charlemagne and the classical world
Charlemagne had no capital city but in later years often ruled his huge empire from his palace in Aachen, Germany. He was a ruler with a great interest in education and culture. Besides his own Frankish language he also spoke Latin. He understood Greek but never learned to write it.

Both in Charlemagne's time and during the reigns of later Carolingian kings, monks were encouraged to study manuscripts that had survived from the Roman and Greek worlds and to make new copies of them. It is because of this that we are now able to read the "classics."

△ A bronze statue of Charlemagne from Metz. Pope Leo III crowned him Emperor of the West on Christmas Day 800.

▷ The back cover of the Lindau Gospels was decorated with gold, silver-gilt and enamel in Charlemagne's time. The decoration of the intertwining animals is earlier.

◁△ Impressive religious buildings and objects show how important Christian worship was at this time. Left, the Carolingian church of a monastery at Corvey in northern Germany. Above, a 9th-century enamel cross, now in the Vatican.

SUTTON HOO

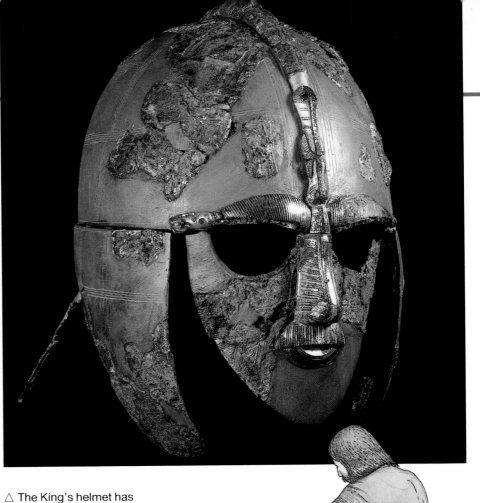

In 1938 the owner of some large barrows (mounds of earth) in Suffolk, England, wanted to find out what was inside. She asked the local museum to find her an excavator. The following year one of the most spectacular archaeological discoveries of the century was made.

The burial of a king

Inside the largest barrow they found the traces of a wooden boat 89 feet long. Although the body had long since rotted away, it had been surrounded with many beautiful and priceless objects. The archaeologists believed that this was the grave of an East Anglian king called Raedwald who died in about 625. Raedwald was also declared *Bretwalda* or High King of Britain. Although the type of burial was pagan (not Christian), Raedwald was buried with some Christian objects. Possibly, he had been converted to the Christian religion.

△ The King's helmet has been reconstructed by specialists at the British Museum. It carries two emblems – a dragon over the crest and a bird across the face. The helmet and the sword and shield are similar to ones found in Sweden. Other objects show how far people traveled at the time – silver dishes from Constantinople were among the possessions of this English chief.

△▷ The King was laid out ready for his journey to the next world in a seagoing clinker-built ship. He had supplies of clothes (cloaks and leather shoes), spears and other weapons and objects ranging from a lyre (a small harp) to a great bronze cauldron.

VIKING EXPANSION

The ravaging of heathens destroyed God's church at Lindisfarne, with much plunder and slaughter.

The Vikings (the "heathens" written about above) were robbers who came by sea – pirates. This quotation is from the *Anglo-Saxon Chronicle*, a history of England put together in the 9th century. This entry is for 793. Many people had every reason to be frightened of these "wolves to be feared" as their warships sailed from their homelands in Scandinavia.

Vikings at home

Vikings were actually several different peoples who lived in what we now know as Norway, Sweden and Denmark. Many people think of them today just as warlike raiders. Not all Vikings were like that. They were farmers, great traders and town builders. Their artists and craftspeople produced beautiful objects.

The search for new lands

Many Vikings set off from their homelands in search of new lands to settle and farm, such as Iceland. Other voyages were carried out for plunder first, then for settlement. Norwegian Vikings began to settle in the islands off the north coast of Scotland at the beginning of the 8th century. From there they moved down the west coast of Britain and across to Ireland.

The Danish Vikings plundered Lindisfarne on the northeast coast of Britain and later East Anglia. Vikings from Sweden moved across the Baltic Sea into eastern Europe. Traveling by river, they eventually reached Constantinople, attacking it in 860.

By the 9th century Viking merchant-warriors had built up a large trading network across the Baltic Sea, linking Europe from end to end.

Plunder, slaves and trade

The Viking raiders certainly looked for and collected plunder but they also required slaves – they called them *thralls*. Some peoples they attacked were forced to buy them off with gold. Trade was important too. For example, a Viking prince established a trading contract by force with Constantinople in 907. The Vikings supplied slaves, timber, furs and honey in exchange for gold, silver and luxury goods.

Ships and the sea

The Vikings were great shipbuilders and sailors. This was the key to their success as traders, raiders and settlers. They made very long voyages in fast ships, even crossing from Iceland to Greenland to settle in North America. Their ships, built with overlapping timber planks, were powered by sails and oars. The Vikings built not only "longships" for raiding (holding up to 200 warriors) but also wider trading ships called *knarrs* and little rowing boats called *faerings*.

△ Reconstruction of a ship excavated from a royal burial mound at Oseberg near Oslo in Norway.

▽ Across the Altantic. The search for new lands and an escape from murderous feuds took some Vikings far overseas. By about 1000 they had reached as far as Labrador and Newfoundland and built settlements there.

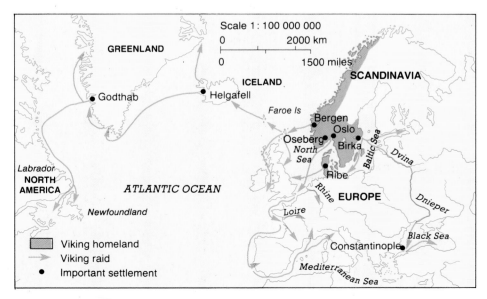

Scale 1 : 100 000 000

Viking homeland
Viking raid
Important settlement

△ A drawing of a Viking farmhouse at Stöng in Iceland, based on archaeological excavations. Viking settlements here were destroyed by a volcanic eruption in 1104. The farm buildings were made of turf and consisted of hall, living room, dairy and lavatory.

▽ Viking settlements in Iceland and Greenland. Sheep farming was the basis of the Vikings' new northern settlements. Written records from these lands show the settlers as hardy and sometimes violent people, feuding and fighting. Some ventured even further west – to the North American coast.

▷ Raids on Britain. Invasions of Vikings were difficult to stop. The Anglo-Saxon King Alfred halted them in 886 and reoccupied London. But a large area of Britain – known as the Danelaw – fell under Viking control. Not until the mid-10th century were they fully overcome.

	Danish Viking settlement (Danelaw)
	Norwegian Viking settlement
→	Viking raid
●	Important settlement

Scale 1 : 7 500 000

0 ——— 150 km

0 ——— 100 miles

Shetland Is

Orkney Is

Hebrides

North Sea

SCOTLAND

Lindisfarne

NORTHUMBRIA

Carlisle

BRITAIN

Heversham

York

IRELAND

Dublin

Isle of Man

ENGLAND

Lincoln

Nottingham

Norwich

Leicester

EAST ANGLIA

MERCIA

Worcester

Wexford

Severn

Pembroke

Thames

London

WESSEX

Canterbury

Winchester

To Normandy

English Channel

Baffin

GREENLAND

ICELAND

Denmark Strait

Holar

Mooruvellir

Davis Strait

Holsteinsborg

Helgafell

Stöng

Thykkvibaer

Angmagssalik

Western settlement

Godthab

Hudson Strait

Resolution

Frederikshab

Gardar

Eastern settlement

Nain

Labrador

ATLANTIC OCEAN

Goose Bay

NORTH AMERICA

Battle Harbour

Bonne Esperance

Gulf of St Lawrence

Newfoundland

St John's

→	Viking raid
	Possible area of Viking settlement
	Permanent ice cover
●	Important settlement

Scale 1 : 24 000 000

0 ——— 600 km

0 ——— 400 miles

THE BYZANTINE EMPIRE

Today we use the word Byzantine to describe the East Roman Empire and Byzantium for the city of Constantinople. Constantine the Great, the Christian Emperor of Rome, made this ancient city (Byzantium) the capital of the East Roman Empire in 330. You have read earlier (page 16) how some parts of the West Roman Empire were lost to various barbarians, such as the Vandals, and how the Emperor Justinian later won back some territory.

The threat from the east

The greatest threat to the Byzantine Empire – the Holy Christian Empire – was from the Muslims in the East. Their religion was Islam, following their prophet Muhammad who lived in the 7th century. By the 8th century they had occupied not only the Middle East but north Africa, Spain and Portugal. The Byzantines held out against Islam, however. In the 9th century, under emperors from Macedonia in northern Greece, they began to push the Muslims back into Syria, and they later conquered the Bulgars in the north.

Constantinople

From the time of the first Macedonian emperors in 867, for about two centuries, Constantinople flourished. The Greek Orthodox Church began to send out missionaries to convert the unbelievers to Christianity. The empire grew. Its capital city, Constantinople, also grew within the walls built by the Emperor Theodosius in the 5th century. The modern Turkish city there, called Istanbul, now fills the area laid out by Theodosius.

The Byzantine Empire lasted until 1453 when the Ottoman Turks conquered its capital.

Revival of the East Roman (Byzantine) Empire

11 May 330 Constantinople founded.
717-41 Reign of Emperor Leo III, who drives off Muslim attacks.
867 Beginning of reign of Basil I, first of the Macedonian emperors.
976-1025 Reign of Emperor Basil II, who conquers the Bulgars. Byzantine Empire at full extent by the end of his reign.
1176 Turkish Seljuks defeat the Byzantine Emperor Manuel I.
23 May 1453 Ottoman Turks take Constantinople. Byzantine Empire collapses.

▽ The Byzantine Empire, showing its fullest extent by about 1025. The people known as the Bulgars were converted to the Orthodox Christian religion in 864, and their territory was conquered in 1018.

Byzantine Empire boundary
--- 867
— 976
-- Temporary acquisition, 970–1000

▢ Maximum extent of Bulgar state, 986

▢ Maximum extent of Byzantine Empire, c.1025

■ Capital city
● Other settlement

Scale 1 : 16 000 000

0   400 km

0   300 miles

▷ The Roman Emperor Justinian built the magnificent new church of Santa Sophia (it means Holy Wisdom) in Constantinople in 537. This is a view of it in 1852 by the architect Fossati, who was commissioned by the Turkish sultan to restore it. It had been converted to an Islamic mosque in 1453.

△ This little drawing of Constantinople, made in 1436, shows the great domed roof of the church of Santa Sophia and a statue of the Emperor Justinian on a horse.

THE PLANTAGENET EMPIRE

The Empire of Charlemagne (page 20) had stretched across the countries we now know as France, Italy and West Germany. His empire was eventually divided into three parts for his grandsons in 843. By this time there were also other divisions of territory created by powerful lords – dukes and counts – who had small armies to control their own lands.

Saxon England

Since the Roman period England had been invaded and settled by different groups, first the Saxons, then the Danes. By the mid-11th century the king was Edward the Confessor, descended from Saxon and Norman families. On his death in 1066 there was no adult male in his family to succeed him. Harold Godwine, the Earl of Wessex and the King's brother-in-law, claimed the throne.

Normandy and England

However, William, Duke of Normandy, had other ideas. He invaded England in 1066, winning the Battle of Hastings and the throne of England. From then the histories of France and England were linked together, and the English king played an important part in continental affairs. Over the next 140 years England and Normandy were usually ruled by one person, although at times the two countries were split between different kings.

The Plantagenet family

The Angevin family, whose base was at Anjou in France, are called Plantagenets by historians. In December 1154 Henry II, the 21-year-old son of Matilda of England and Geoffrey of Anjou, came to England as king after the death of his cousin Stephen. He was already Duke of Normandy and of Aquitaine. He then led expeditions far into neighboring territories (building strong castles to impose his control) and increased the Plantagenet Empire. The lands he eventually controlled stretched from the borders of Scotland to the Pyrenees, but this "empire" was not to last.

▷ The Plantagenet Empire. The empire was bordered on the east by the lands of the king of France and on the south by various lordships. Henry II moved about his territory even when he was not fighting. He spent most of his time close to hunting reserves and frontiers – the Thames Valley, Southampton, Barfleur and the Seine Valley.

◁ Henry II had a number of strong, stone castles built, especially along coasts which were open to attack. In England, Dover Castle was built by Henry II (although it has been added to over the years). So was Orford Castle in Suffolk, pictured here. Orford Castle took eight years to complete at a cost of more than £1,400 – a fortune in the 12th century. The keep, the strongest part, and some earthworks still survive.

Linlithgow ▲
▲ Edinburgh
Berwick
Kelso
▲ Roxburgh
Ayr ▲
SCOTLAND
Dumfries ▲
● Newcastle ▲
Carlisle ▲
North Sea
Richmond ▲
Lancaster ▲
York ●
Pontefract ▲
Conisborough ▲
Deganwy
Lincoln ●
Rhuddlan ▲
Beaumaris ▲ ● Chester ▲
Caernarvon ▲ Conway ▲ Hawarden ▲
ENGLAND
Shrewsbury ●
Leicester ●
Norwich ●
WALES
Coventry ●
Aberystwyth ▲
Orford ▲
Cardigan ▲ Builth ●
Hereford ●
Colchester ●
Pembroke ▲
Llandaff ●
London ▲
Thames
Canterbury ▲
Wells ●
Dover ▲
Salisbury ●
Southampton ● Winchester ● Chichester ● Hastings ●
Exeter ●
English Channel

Armagh ●
Granard ▲
Tuam ●
Athlone ▲
Dublin ▲
IRELAND
Birr ▲
Trimahoe ▲ Athy ▲
Limerick ▲ Leighlin ▲
Cashel ●
Ardfinnan ▲
Lismore ▲ Waterford ▲

ATLANTIC
OCEAN

Bay of Biscay

Barfleur ●
Seine
Rouen ●
Château Gaillard ▲
Bayeux ●
NORMANDY
Evreux ●
St Pol de Léon ●
St Malo ●
Avranches ●
St Brieuc ●
MAINE
FRANCE
BRITTANY
Le Mans ●
Rennes ●
Tours ●
Bourges ●
Vannes ●
Loire
Chinon ▲
Nantes ●
ANJOU
Loudun ▲
TOURAINE
POITOU
Mirbeau ▲
Poitiers ●
LA MARCHE
Clermont-Ferrand ●
Saintes ●
AUVERGNE
AQUITAINE
VELAY
Périgueux ●
Bordeaux ●
Garonne
Mende ●
Cahors ●
Uzès ●
QUERCY
Agen ●
Albi ●
Lodève ●
GASCONY
Aire ● TOULOUSE
Béziers ●
Bayonne ●
Auch ●
Toulouse ●
Maguelone ●
Lescar ●
Narbonne ●
Oloron ●
Comminges ●
NAVARRE
FOIX
Mediterranean Sea
PYRENEES
ARAGON

Legend:
— Boundary of Plantagenet Empire, 1154
Ruled by Stephen until 1154
Ruled by Henry II from 1149
Acquired by Henry II, 1151
Acquired by Henry II, 1152
Acquired by Henry II, 1154–1189
Disputed land
‐ ‐ ‐ Boundary of Plantagenet Empire in France, 1226
Toulouse, 1154
▲ Castle
● Other settlement

Scale 1 : 5 000 000
0   150 km
0   100 miles

Plantagenet power

In France: Henry II becomes Duke of Normandy **1149**, Count of Anjou **1151** and Duke of Aquitaine **1152**.

England in 1154: Stephen is King of England until his death in **1154** (Duke of Normandy 1135–44). Henry II becomes King.

Campaigns:
  1157, 1163, 1165 Wales.
  1159 Toulouse. **1166** Britanny.

New territories acquired: **1159** Quercy.
  1171 Britanny (by the marriage of Henry II's son, Geoffrey).
  1171 Henry is recognized as lord in Ireland and in Scotland in **1174** but never rules there.

THE BAYEUX TAPESTRY

The famous Bayeux Tapestry is an exciting account in pictures and in words of the events that led to the successful Norman invasion of England in 1066.

It begins: "EDWARD REX. UBI HAROLD DUX ANGLORUM ET SUI MILITES EQUITANT AD BOSHAM." This text, in Latin, provides the caption for the picture-story. It means "Edward the King. Where Harold, Duke of the English, and his soldiers ride to Bosham."

Harold and William

When Edward, King of England, died in 1066 there were two powerful leaders who claimed the throne – Harold and William, Duke of Normandy. At the beginning of the tapestry we learn that Harold traveled to Normandy and swore to support William. But as soon as Edward died Harold claimed the English throne. William prepared for invasion and war in England. He built a great fleet and on September 28 sailed to Pevensey in Sussex on the south coast of England. The Normans landed their army, horses and supplies and then built a timber-and-earth castle at Hastings. Meanwhile Harold hurried south after defeating King Harald of Norway near York.

▽ The Bayeux Tapestry is not really a tapestry at all, because it was not woven. The pictures and words are embroidered in colored wools on linen. It is over 230ft long and 20in wide. William's half-brother, Bishop Odo of Bayeux, probably ordered it to be made. The work was probably completed in England and then carried across the Channel to be displayed at Bayeux Cathedral, France.

The battle of Hastings

William had an army of about 7,000, including 2,000 cavalrymen. The English army was smaller but fought well at a place later called Battle. The tapestry gives all the gory detail of the battle; arrows and spears fly through the air and men are cut down. Finally Harold is wounded and killed. The English have a Norman king – William the Conqueror.

Rediscovering the tapestry

Although the tapestry remained safe in the cathedral at Bayeux, it was not discovered to be an important historical "document" until the 18th century. It was moved several times during the Second World War, but it is now on display to the public in a special building.

◁ The tapestry is a marvelous source of illustrations of the 11th century. It shows a number of buildings, such as churches, castles and towers. William's invasion fleet has ships built in the Viking style (long and clinker-built).

▽ The battle scenes show us how men fought at the time and the weapons and armor they carried – conical helmets with nose protectors, chain mail, swords and axes. Here King Harold is wounded with a Norman arrow and then cut down.

DOMESDAY BOOK

There are many different kinds of written evidence for the medieval period. They include histories, surveys, laws, court hearings, wills and inventories (lists) of property in houses. Some of these documents have survived and can be studied today.

King William's survey

The Bayeux Tapestry provides evidence for William the Conqueror's invasion of England. Another important document has survived to help us understand what the conquered land of England was like – this time a written record.

In 1086 King William ordered a survey of all his English lands to check that he was receiving

▷ King William, "after much thought and very deep discussion with his council," so the *Anglo-Saxon Chronicle* says, sent commissioners throughout England to collect the information for the Domesday Book. In each village or town a jury had to answer questions about the people and the resources of their lands. Other information collected included the number of clergy and churches.

Terra Epī Herefordenſis.   In Writa.ten& Epc̄.ii.hid̄.7.xx.ac̄.q̄ru̅   XIX.
una fuit in eccła t̄.r̄.e̅.7 alia feudo haroldi.Sep̄.iii.uiłł.7.i.p̄br.Tc̄.ii.bor.
m̄.viii.Tc̄.ii.ſer̄ m̄ nułł.sep̄.i.car̄ in d̄nio.7.ii.car̄ hom̄.ſiłu̅.c.porc̄.viii.
ac̄.p̄ti.Val̄.l.ſol̄.

TERRE Comitis Euſtachij In Exffeſſa.   Hund de berdeſtapla.   .XX.
Phobinge tenuit Brictmar un teinn regis Eaduuardi .p.v.hid̄.7.p uno man̄.
m̄ ten& comes.E.in d̄nio.Sep̄.iiii.car̄ in d̄nio.7.v.carruc̄.hominu̅.Tc̄.viii.uiłł
m̄.iii.Tc̄.viii.bor.m̄.xxii.Tc̄.xii.ſer̄.m̄.vi.Siłu̅.dcc.porc̄.Paſt.dcc.ouib;.dim̄
piſcina.xxxi.porc̄.dcc.ou̅.7 xvii.Ex hac t̄ra tulit Turold.xxx.ac̄.quæ ſt̄
ad feudu̅ ep̄i baiocenſis.Et hoc addidit Ingelric̄ huic manerio.xxii.libos ho̅es
tenentes.xv.hid̄.7.dimid̄.7.xv.ac̄.7.dim̄.In q̄ t̄ra.ſt̄ ſep̄.xii.car̄.7.xx.bord.
7.iii.ſer̄.Siłu̅.l.porc̄.x.ac̄.p̄ti.Paſt.cccc.ou̅.Tcia pars uni piſcinæ.7 poſſt
addi.iii.car̄.7.dim̄.Tc̄ ual̄.manariu̅.xx.lib̄.7 t̄ra.ſochemano₂.xii.lib̄.M
in̄t totu̅.xxxvi.lib̄.
Horninduna̅ ten& Garner̄ de comite q̄d tenuit Vluric lib̄ ho̅.p.uno
manerio.7.p.ii.hid̄.7.l.ac̄.Sep̄.ii.car̄.in d̄nio.Tc̄.ii.uiłł.m̄ nułł.Tc̄.vii.

Translation of the Domesday Book entry (boxed area):
Brictmer, a thane of King Edward's, held FOBBING for 5 hides, as one manor. Now Count Eustace holds it in lordship. Always 4 ploughs in lordship; 5 men's ploughs.

Then 8 villagers, now 3; then 8 smallholders, now 22; then 12 slaves, now 6.

Woodland, 700 pigs; pasture, 700 sheep; ½ fishery. 31 pigs, 717 sheep.

all the rents and taxes to which he was entitled. This survey came to be known as the Domesday Book and was referred to for many years afterwards. In fact, there are two volumes of records. The Great Domesday surveys most of England, while the Little Domesday covers only the counties of Essex, Norfolk and Suffolk. Not every place was recorded – the towns of Winchester and London, and large parts of the north of England, were left out.

What is recorded?
King William wanted a record of who owned the land at the time of his invasion of England in 1066 and who held the land 20 years later, in 1086. The Domesday Book records this as *then* (before 1066) and *now* (in 1086). It states that William gave land to friends, such as Odo, the Bishop of Bayeux, who fought with him at Hastings. It also records the number of plow teams a village had. Most of the population were "villeins" and "bordars," who were villagers who held varying amounts of land in the estate or village. "Slaves" were owned by the lord and had no land for themselves.

The Domesday Book also gives some information about animals and the amount of land available for feeding and pasturing animals. If the village had other resources, such as fishponds, mills, beehives and salt-works, they too were recorded.

△ The entry in the Domesday Book for the village of Fobbing in Essex tells us that Brictmer was lord of the manor under the Saxon king Edward the Confessor. King William gave Fobbing to Eustace, Count of Boulogne, who fought at the Battle of Hastings. The entry shows that in 1066 there were eight villeins (tenants), in 1086 only three, and so on. The entry finishes with a list of other resources.

◁ An aerial photograph of Onley, Northamptonshire, a village in medieval times, now deserted except for a modern farm on the site. What you can see are the earthworks – the only remains of fields, gardens, houses and streets. The most striking feature is the way the fields were plowed in strips leaving furrows on each side. Around the barn in the center of the photograph is the village itself with "hollow ways," or deeply cut tracks, running through it. On each side are the individual plots of land for the villagers.

THE CRUSADES

In the areas of Europe that had become Christian – Christendom is the general name often used – there were many devout followers of the religion. Religious "orders" were set up, and followers lived in religious communities of monks and nuns. Special religious objects (such as the bones of a saint) and holy places (shrines) were treated with great respect. From the 4th century, within the Roman Empire people made special journeys called pilgrimages to these holy places.

The Holy Land of Palestine was the most important destination for pilgrims. But the shrines of St Peter and St Paul in Rome became popular among pilgrims, especially after Jerusalem was taken by the Muslims in 638.

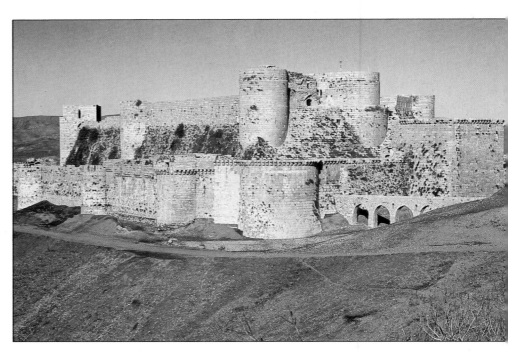

The Holy Land – lost to Christians

The Arab Muslims, followers of the prophet Muhammad, did not stop Christians from visiting the Holy Land. However, in 1076 Turkish Muslims captured Jerusalem from the Arabs. They turned Christians away, arresting and torturing some pilgrims. The Christian emperor in Constantinople called for help in fighting these Turks.

Fighting for Christ

To help the emperor, Pope Urban II in 1095 called for a "crusade" ("war of the cross") to win back the Holy Land from the "unbelievers." Huge numbers joined the cause and "took up the cross." The First Crusade won back Jerusalem within four years. Other crusades followed. There were many problems – not only in fighting the enemy but between the "Latin" Christians, who were led by Rome, and the "Greek" or "Orthodox" Christians, whose capital was Constantinople.

△ Krak des Chevaliers in Syria, a huge castle built by crusaders. Crusading knights formed into different "orders." Krak was held by the Knights of St John the Hospitalers (they were dedicated to defending the sick) from 1142 to 1271.

The Crusades: success and failure

First Crusade 1095: 1095 Crusade called for in the West by Pope Urban II. **1096** Crusaders reach Constantinople. **1098** Antioch besieged and captured. **1099** Jerusalem captured.
Second Crusade 1145: 1145 Edessa lost. Crusade achieves nothing.
Third Crusade 1189: 1174 Saladin, Sultan of Egypt, captures Damascus, **1183** Aleppo, **1187** Jerusalem. **1189** Crusade led by Emperor Frederick of Germany, King Richard I ("Lionheart") of England and King Philip II of France. Coastal towns and forts recaptured.
Children's Crusade 1212: Several thousand children go on crusade. Those who reach Alexandria are sold as slaves.
Crusade of 1248: Led by Louis IX of France, who is captured by the Egyptians and ransomed.

▷ Crusader states. The crusaders set about founding states in the Holy Land that could be held against the "unbelievers" and be organized like those in western Europe.

◁ A crusading army led by knights on horseback besieges a Muslim castle. Footsoldiers fought with spears and crossbows, and large siege-engines were also used. These included mangonels, which hurled great stones at the walls and could kill as many as twelve men with its blows.

▲ Castle
◆ Fortified city
● Other settlement

Places under the control of
● Knights Templar
● Teutonic Knights
● Knights of St John the Hospitallers

al-Marqab
Masyaf
Orontes
Tartus
Krak des Chevaliers
Homs
Tripoli
Jubail
Baalbek
Beirut
Damascus
Sidon
Litani
Sarafand
HOLY LAND
Belfort
Tyre
Subeiba
Banyas
Toron
OF
Scandalion
Montfort
Sumeriya
Acre
Juddin
Safad
Mediterranean Sea
L Tiberias
Recordane
Qasr Bardawi
Haifa
Nazareth
Tiberias
Athlith
Caymont
ISRAEL
Merle
Afrabala
Belvoir
Caesarea
Sabarim
Bethsan
Jenin
Qaqun
Letaria
Ajlun
Qaloniya
Nablus
Jordan
Arsuf
Jaffa
Mirabel
Yazur
Ramla
al-Bira
Ibelin
Yalu
Jerusalem
Huldre
Bethlehem
Ascalon
Bothme
Beth Gibelin
Gaza
Agelen
Hebron
Dead Sea
Darum
al-Samoa
Karak
Shaubak
Wadi Musa

Scale 1 : 2 000 000
0   60 km
0   40 miles

COUNTY OF EDESSA 1098–1145
Edessa
Antioch
Aleppo
PRINCIPALITY OF ANTIOCH 1098–1268
Area covered by main map
Tripoli
COUNTY OF TRIPOLI 1109–1289
Mediterranean Sea
Tyre
Damascus
Jerusalem
Crusader states
After 1st Crusade
KINGDOM OF JERUSALEM 1099–1187
Scale 1 : 12 500 000

Edessa
Antioch
Aleppo
Area covered by main map
Tripoli
Mediterranean Sea
Tyre
Damascus
Jerusalem
Saladin's conquests
Before 3rd Crusade
Scale 1 : 12 500 000

THE GERMAN EMPIRE

The West Roman Empire had a long and complicated history. Previous maps show how it emerged from earlier empires to become the most important state in Europe. From 962 it was called the Holy Roman Empire. Earlier in this period it is sometimes called the Saxon Empire, as it was ruled by Saxon kings. The rulers of the empire were all Germans.

King Henry of Germany

The lands of Germany were divided into duchies, lands belonging to dukes. Each duke was powerful and had his own army and castles. They did recognize kings but often fought against them. In 919 Henry, Duke of Saxony, succeeded the previous king, Conrad of Franconia. At first Henry had authority over only these two areas but he was eventually recognized as Henry I throughout Germany.

Enemies on the borders

The Germans had two main enemies – the Magyars (Hungarians) and the Slavs. Henry I tricked the Magyars into a truce while he built castles and fortress towns, such as Quedlinburg and Merseburg. In the war of 933 he beat these enemies. The Slavs were more difficult as they had settled in large numbers and were farming lands north of the River Elbe. Gradually, though, the German kings extended their territory eastwards.

Otto I – emperor

Henry's son Otto came to the throne in 936. He made the German dukes his subjects. One writer at the time said that the dukes "gave him their lands and promised him their loyalty and help against all enemies." Otto attacked the Magyars and finally defeated them in 955. He extended his authority in other ways too. In 951 he became King of Italy and he was crowned Holy Roman Emperor in 962.

The Holy Roman Empire

Otto saw himself as the natural successor to the Emperor Charlemagne. His title was Imperator Augustus – Emperor Augustus. In 998 his grandson Otto III proclaimed that the old Roman Empire was now revived. The people of Rome itself, however, never really liked these German emperors and rose up against him.

◁ Scenes from the life of Pope Gregory VII (1073-85), from the Bishop of Freising's *World Chronicle*. The Emperor Henry IV of Germany campaigned in Italy against the Pope. These four scenes describe the dispute, showing more sympathy for Gregory (top center and again right) than for Henry (top left). They also give an early example of how history could be tellingly depicted by pictures from this period.

△ The German Empire (Holy Roman Empire). The main boundaries show how the empire grew.

German Empire
Boundary, c.962
Regional boundary, c.962
Duchy
Associated state
March
Boundary, 1158
Slavs Name of people
◆ Fortress town
• Other settlement

Scale 1 : 6 500 000

0 — 100 km
0 — 75 miles

◁ Drawing from a manuscript of 1425 showing a panmaker at work in Nuremburg, Germany. The panmaker is using a pointed hammer to pierce the bowl-shaped metal utensil repeatedly to produce a colander for straining. A medieval kitchen would contain all the cooking utensils we know today.

△ The German Empire (Holy Roman Empire). The main boundaries show how the empire grew. The kingdoms of Italy and Burgundy were absorbed in the 10th and 11th centuries, but the Lombards of northern Italy were always troublesome. Noble families and princes became increasingly powerful in Germany itself.

A March was a frontier territory often disputed with the neighboring kingdom or country. It was heavily militarized at all times. A Duchy was a territory controlled by a duke (or duchess) and with its own laws. Associated states were, at various times, ruled by their own kings.

German expansion

919-36 Henry I is King of Germany. Campaigns against the Slavs and Magyars.
955 Otto I finally defeats the Magyars.
967-70 Attempts to gain territory in southern Italy.
1033 Kingdom of Burgundy added to empire.
1158 Kingdom of Bohemia added to empire.
1158 March of Lausitz, **1163** Duchy of Silesia, Opol and Ratibor and **1181** Duchy of Pomerania under German control.
1194 Kingdom of Sicily acquired by Henry VI.
1231 Teutonic Knights win Prussia.

THE MEDIEVAL CHURCH

The Christian Church developed slowly at first in the Roman world. By the 3rd century Christianity was spreading quickly. Bishops were in charge of Christian worship in communities all over the Roman Empire. Being a Christian was not always easy in the Roman world, but after 312 Christians were not persecuted for their religion. Christianity finally became the "official" religion of the Roman Empire in 395 under the Emperor Theodosius.

Christian monks

The word "monk" comes from a Greek word for alone – *monos*. The first Christian monks lived alone, away from other communities, in the Egyptian desert. The first religious communities of nuns were also established in Egypt. Monks and nuns did not marry and lived apart from all comforts and luxuries.

The idea of the monastic life spread through the Roman world – not only in the eastern Mediterranean but also in north Africa, Italy, Gaul (France), Britain and beyond the Roman provinces in Ireland.

Medieval monasteries

After the Roman period many monasteries were founded that followed the Rule (or code) of St Benedict. Other "orders" of monks and nuns were also established. For example, a community was established in 909 at Cluny in Burgundy. By the next century there were 1,450 Cluniac communities established throughout western Europe.

The organization of Christianity

The system of organizing Christianity for the community was set up in the Roman period. Bishops were appointed to areas called dioceses. Priests or vicars served individual communities in parishes within dioceses. A church was built for each community, but its size and structure depended upon what each parish could afford. The shape and architecture of the parish church varied enormously across the Christian world. In theory all Western religious communities looked to Rome and the pope as the central authority. Often, though, communities acted as they thought best.

△ An illustrated letter B from a Bible now in Winchester, England. The Bible was made for the Bishop of Winchester, Henry of Blois, in the late 12th century. Part of the picture shows Jesus driving out devils.

▷ This 12th-century illustration shows a monk making a copy of the Bible. Bibles were beautifully illustrated by monks. These hand-made books were highly treasured, and only a few survive today from the early periods.

△ ▷ The church at Wroxeter in Shropshire, England, stands in one corner of a Roman town, most of which is now hidden under grass fields. There may have been a Christian community here in the Roman period.

In the 9th century a decorated Anglo-Saxon cross must have stood in the churchyard (above). Parts of this cross survive in the wall of the aisle of the church. Crosses were centers for worship.

Most parish churches in Britain have a long history (right). There may have been a church here even before the one built in the 7th or 8th century. The Anglo-Saxon builders used large stones from the Roman town to construct their nave and chancel. The Domesday Book (pages 32-33) records four priests here in 1086.

Tower

Nave

Aisle

Chancel

Chapel

Porch

800-900

1200

1300

1400

△ ▷ The church at Wroxeter today has additions from many centuries. Now the entrance is through the 19th-century porch. Porches in the medieval period were often used to conduct parish business.

The aisle allowed more people to be in the congregation at services, and there was often a chapel in the aisle (as here) built by a wealthy person as a place for the priest to pray for the soul.

The nave was where the congregation stood (there were usually no seats in a medieval church). The chancel was where the priest conducted the service. The tower had the bells to summon the people to the service.

This view of Wroxeter Church (right) shows the Anglo-Saxon nave and the tower.

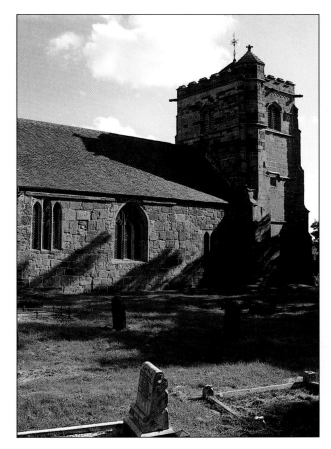

EDUCATION

In the medieval period, for most people education or learning, either reading or writing, served no practical purpose. There were many people – both workers and the wealthy – who could not read or write. But the clergy in the churches did need to be educated.

Literature from earlier periods

Manuscripts from the Romans (and a few Greek ones) survived long enough for monks to copy them out and to study them. Not all those involved in religion were educated. But clergy who served country parishes needed skills in reading, writing and music, as few children were able to attend schools.

Schools

Schools were established for children, either as part of monasteries or by the bishop. For example, Lanfranc, appointed Archbishop of Canterbury, England, in 1070, set up a school at Canterbury for local children. Parish priests also did some teaching. The 12th-century historian Ordericus Vitalis was sent to a priest in Shrewsbury, England, at the age of five and

learned reading, grammar and music before taking holy orders to become a monk.

Universities

Places where students could continue their studies longer were being established by the church from the 12th century onwards. The most famous universities were at Paris (for philosophy and religion), Bologna in northern Italy (for law) and Salerno in southern Italy (for medicine). In England, the first colleges were established in Oxford and Cambridge in the 13th century.

◁ Nicholas of Lyra, seen teaching here in the center, was a monk from Normandy who taught at the University of Paris in the 14th century. Like most other teachers he gave lectures to his students in a very formal way.

▷ Hugh of St Victor teaching in his monastery at St Victor in Paris. Hugh became the prior, or leader, of the college in 1133. This was a college of canons who followed the Rule of St Augustine. A canon was a clerk who lived according to a Rule (the word in Greek for "rule" is *kanon*). The illustration here is from one of Hugh's own works in a manuscript edition made in the 13th century. This copy is now in the Bodleian Library of Oxford University, England.

◁ The medieval university of Bologna, northern Italy, was grouped in two areas, close to each other, inside the walls of the city. The famous law school was in the center. The building you can see here, in the center of the medieval university area, is the Palazzo of King Enzo built in 1246 and used as his prison for 23 years until his death in 1272. The university grew very fast during these years.

CATHEDRAL BUILDING

We know that cathedrals are usually large, grand churches, but the word itself can be traced back to the Romans. In Latin *cathedra* means professor's or teacher's chair. The word was used in the medieval period in exactly the same way – both Hugh and Nicholas are illustrated seated at their cathedral on pages 40-41. The word for "seat" becomes "important church" because a cathedral was where the seat or throne of the bishop of the diocese was.

Size and shape
Cathedrals are usually large, but it is possible to find some ordinary parish churches in England, for example, which are larger than cathedrals. A cathedral was also either secular (served by canons who were clerks) or monastic (served by monks). A secular cathedral building would stand on its own like a big church.

A monastic cathedral would be a church building attached to a whole group of other buildings for the monks to live and work in. There would be, for example, a chapter house (for daily meetings, announcements and sometimes punishments), a refectory (dining room), an infirmary (hospital), kitchens, a dormitory (large room for sleeping), a lavatorium (for washing) and a reredorter (lavatory).

A new style of building
In the middle of the 12th century in France a completely new style of church building was developed. The Gothic style with its elaborate architecture and glass-filled windows allowed the building dedicated to God to be filled with "the new light," as one writer put it.

These buildings were very expensive and often took many years to complete. Gervase, a monk at the cathedral church at Canterbury, England, wrote in 1174:

The master-mason, William of Sens, began to prepare all that was necessary for the new building and to destroy what was there before. This took the first year. In the next year he put up four pillars and after the winter two more ...

A master-mason might work with about 30 experienced craftsmen who traveled from job to job. Local people would be brought in for the unskilled jobs, such as carrying stone.

Columns, aisles and arches
This new style of architecture involved new types of building techniques, which the planners and masons (stonecutters) had to invent and test. The techniques did not always work – occasionally buildings fell down.

Cathedrals needed to hold large congregations of people but they had to look as if they were worthy to be called "houses for God." The builders of Gothic architecture were the first to discover how to put up very tall buildings of stone without enormously thick walls to carry all that weight. This discovery allowed them to design and build churches that looked beautiful both inside and out.

▽ Cathedral building required great blocks of stone. Two types of crane are shown here – the winch (left) and the treadwheel (right).

▷ It took a lot of skill to be a mason, cutting and carving stone accurately.

◁ This cutaway drawing shows that the inside of the cathedral is made bigger by aisles of columns on each side. Compare the building's size with that of the people on the ground.

▽ The extraordinary height of Gothic cathedrals is possible because of these "flying buttresses," which help carry the weight of the building outside on columns and arches.

▽ Part of the strength of these buildings was in their vaulted arches. They were constructed of stone over a wooden frame that was taken away when the stone construction was finished.

▷ In France the new Chartres Cathedral was rebuilt after a fire in 1194. The money for this large Gothic building came from four trade fairs held each year on feast days of the Virgin Mary. A special feature of cathedrals from the 12th century is the huge rose window of stained glass.

STORIES IN STAINED GLASS

The church shines, with its middle part brightened.

The "new light" described by Abbot Suger, the leader of a community of monks in the early 12th century, was brought about in churches and cathedrals by the lightness of the building, towering to the sky, and by the light that streamed in through the windows. Not just white light came in – the light was made all the colors of the rainbow by stained glass.

Creating an atmosphere

Churches and cathedrals were built to honor God. Those responsible for the building may have wanted to show how wealthy and powerful they were, but it was even more important to create the right atmosphere for those who came to worship. Gothic buildings, as we have seen, were very impressive buildings – it is almost impossible not to wonder at them.

The atmosphere inside the church was created by sculpture, paintings and the elaborate ceremonies full of chanting and music. Perhaps even more important was the "feel" created by the stained glass all around. Like the glittering effect of Byzantine mosaics, stained glass helped the worshipers to feel they really were in a special place.

Stories in the window

Many people could not read so they were unable to discover for themselves the stories in the Bible or to learn from them, as their priests wanted them to. Stained glass, and also wall paintings, allowed them to "read" the stories for themselves. In many cases, however, it would be difficult to get more than just an impression of the story in windows high up in cathedrals. The story of Christ's life, and especially his death, was a favorite subject. The saints (there were a great number of them in the medieval world) and their lives were often pictured.

Making a window

It is easy to appreciate from the pictures shown here that making stained-glass windows was a skilled job. Glass was made from a mixture of ash from the wood of beech trees and washed sand heated to a very high temperature. The color produced was greenish and it was difficult to see through. To produce bright colors different kinds of metal, such as iron and copper oxides, were added to the mixture.

The glass was cut into small pieces and joined together to make up the picture with little strips of lead. Lines of paint were also added to produce a picture in glass. Sections of these leaded pictures were held together with iron rods and fitted into the carved stone window frames.

Chartres

One of the best buildings in which to see stained glass is Chartres Cathedral in northern France. Most of the medieval windows there still survive.

▷ A 12th-century window at Chartres Cathedral. Between 1200 and 1235 more than 100 stained-glass windows were made. This work was paid for by a variety of people – from King Louis IX to the Count of Brittany and from the rich merchants in the city to the masons who worked on the building. The scenes here are from Christ's last days – for example, the Last Supper and washing the feet of his disciples (at the bottom).

△ This window is a good example of a rose window. This one is in the church of Notre-Dame (Our Lady) in Paris. It was made by two craftsmen in about 1270. The shape of the window and the colors used allow light to sparkle through into the church.

▷ A chapel window in Strasbourg Cathedral, in France, made in the mid-14th century. Later windows such as this were made using the technique of painting on larger sheets of glass. The scenes here show the Resurrection of Christ.

MEDIEVAL ARTS AND CRAFTS

One of the most extraordinary aspects of the medieval period in Europe is the range of works of art created by skilled craftspeople. Decoration was everywhere, from the complicated fronts of cathedrals to the metal clasps on Bibles. All sorts of techniques were used, such as carving in stone and wood, metalwork, painting, stained-glass and tapestry making.

Builders in stone...

You have seen before how stonemasons were used to create cathedrals to be wondered at. Sculptors provided decoration for both the inside and outside of these buildings – on windows, columns and towers. Doorways especially were often highly decorated with intricate carvings of birds, horses and leaves. Medieval cathedrals also had a great number of carvings of individual people in niches (indentations in walls), especially about people from the Bible, saints, popes and kings.

...and in wood

Wood does not survive as well as stone, but there are still a great many examples of the medieval woodworker's craft. Wood was very important in building, especially up to the 12th century. Even after that most ordinary buildings were of wood. Skills were developed to create complex constructions in wood. A manuscript describes the new wooden tower of Ely Cathedral, England, in 1328 as

> *the ingenious wooden structure, designed with great and astonishing subtlety ... huge beams cut and cunningly made into frames for the work by clever craftsmen.*

Writers

We have already seen some examples of literature from the medieval period. Historians have left us information about people and events in the past. There were also many poems and stories. The clergy wrote mainly in Latin, but gradually the languages that people spoke were used for literature too.

Stories that retold tales from the classical (Greek and Roman) periods were very popular. So was heroic poetry, usually recited aloud, praising the skills and exploits of warriors. Here is a short translated extract from *Beowulf*, a

◁ Early surviving examples of wood carving, such as this small figure of the Virgin Mary from the church at Griske, Sunnøre, Norway, show that craftsmen of the period had already acquired great expressive power.

▷ A pattern book made in about 1380 showing various birds (the bullfinch is labeled). Pattern books were used by designers, wood carvers and people doing embroidery.

▽ The wooden roof of a small parish church in Garway, Herefordshire, England, shows the skill of local carpenters. The roof frames have beams that tie the outside walls together (tie beams), collar beams to hold the frame together and braces.

poem written in Old English in the 8th century about a Germanic hero who overcomes monsters but is finally slain by a dragon.

Then the dragon awoke, anger was renewed; he stalked along the rocks, with brave heart he had found
the fiend's footprints; he had stepped with stealthy craft, near the dragon's head.

Music

Music was very important in medieval life. A special way of singing psalms (chanting) in monasteries was developed and became part of monks' daily services. Plainchants were sung in monasteries from the earliest periods. After the 11th century other lines of melody were added. Outside of religious life, traveling performers known as troubadours recited poetry and tales and sang accompanied by instruments such as trumpets, bagpipes and lutes.

▽ Pope Gregory the Great at his writing desk with his symbol, the dove. He was pope in the 6th century. This beautiful 10th-century carving is made of ivory (animal tusk) and was the cover of a book now in a museum in Vienna, Austria.

▽ This illustration is from a medieval Spanish manuscript and shows two musicians. The manuscript also has some lines of music drawn out (not shown here) to help singers accompany the players.

47

SCIENCE, MEDICINE AND PRINTING

The modern word "science" comes from the Latin word *scientia* meaning "a knowledge of." Classical and medieval people wanted a knowledge of a great many things that they saw around them but did not always understand. Knowledge and inventions from the Greeks and Romans passed to the Eastern Roman Empire in Constantinople.

Muslim technology

Muslims in the East acquired this knowledge and developed it, collecting as much information as they could. For example, an 11th-century author, al-Bakri, says that the caliph (ruler) ordered a full survey to be made of the Roman aqueducts (for providing a regular water supply) in northern Tunisia so that ideas could be gained to develop their own system. The Muslims were skillful observers and recorders, and invented accurate measuring instruments.

Passing on the knowledge

The Christian medieval world often came into contact with Muslims and their knowledge in the 12th century, particularly in Spain and Sicily. Scholars began to go to these countries to learn from, and to translate, the manuscripts they found there.

A number of inventions were very practical, such as the magnetic needle in the compass for navigation or spectacles to discover the science of light. Many ideas were outlined – some ahead of their time, such as the helicopter drawn by Leonardo da Vinci as early as 1486.

Medicine

The science of medicine and healing was well advanced in classical times. In the medieval period, though, herbs were the main source of treatment. Some remedies that doctors used then we do not use today. For example, the medieval treatment of bleeding with a leech (a blood-sucking water worm) probably stopped many people getting better.

Medieval people also believed in God's direct power over their bodies – the Plague was thought to be punishment from God. Their belief in the "influence" of the atmosphere around them to cause sickness gives us the name *influenza*. Folklore, the beliefs passed

◁ Model of a gear and barrel-like spring system invented by Leonardo da Vinci, 1452-1519, the great Italian painter, sculptor, architect, engineer and scientist.

▷ Page from a book on medicine written by a doctor in Baghdad in the 11th century. The text explains how marrows can be used for thirst and to clean out the bowels.

▽ Astrolabes are for observing the sun and the moon and making accurate measurements. The astrolabe shown here was made by a Muslim in Toledo in Spain in 1068.

△ Two 13th-century illustrations to go with a medical text from about 1170. Here a doctor, dressed in the long gown of his profession, examines patients suffering from ailments in the leg and knee.

from generation to generation, played a major part in medicine and healing.

How printing developed

Passing on knowledge was difficult in the medieval world. There were schools and universities, and there were books but these had to be copied out by hand. There was no quick and easy way of reproducing ideas and information. By the 14th century paper not only had been invented but was in good supply. Religious pictures, some with lettering added, could be produced by means of wood blocks (using the same method as a linocut or potato print today).

The first printed book

The next stage was to make individual letters of metal that could be put together to make up a page of text. The inventor seems to have been Johann Gutenberg in the town of Mainz in Germany. The earliest printed book was probably Gutenberg's *Book of Psalms* of 1457. The idea was spread by German printers to Paris, Venice and Rome, and by 1500 there were 250 towns in Europe that had their own printing presses. Venice was an important center, with 150 presses at work there. Knowledge and new ideas soon spread via books throughout Europe in a variety of languages.

△ A printing press in about 1520. The press pushes the inked block onto individual sheets of paper.

▷ Two playing cards printed in about 1470. Printing was not always for serious purposes.

PART TWO

THE LANDS OF MEDIEVAL EUROPE

▷ A 14th-century illustration depicting a scene from *Roman de la Rose*, a medieval love poem by two French writers, de Lorris and de Meung.

TRAVEL

"Whan that Aprille with his shoures sote /
The droghte of Marche hath perced to the
rote..."

*When in April the sweet showers fall and pierce
the drought of March to the root...then people
long to go on pilgrimages.*

This is the opening of a long poem called *The
Canterbury Tales* by Geoffrey Chaucer written
in the late 14th century. The poem is about a
group of people who join together to make the
five-day journey from London to Canterbury to
worship at the shrine of St Thomas à Becket.

During the medieval period all sorts of
people made long journeys, though travel was
not nearly as easy as it is today or even as it was
in the Roman period. Traveling musicians and
actors entertained pilgrims, and others, on the
road and in the inns.

Roads

During the hundreds of years of the Roman
Empire a huge network of roads had been
developed. It allowed the army to move swiftly
from one trouble spot to another. It also allowed
merchants to trade across countries, and news
and ideas to spread. You can still see Roman
roads today, and so they were certainly used by
people in the medieval period. There was no
imperial highway authority to maintain the
roads (as there is today), though local sections
and bridges were looked after and improved.
Tolls (travel taxes) were paid on some roads.

The Canterbury pilgrims did not choose to
travel far, but many pilgrims did. They crossed
Europe to Rome and on to the Holy Land, or to
the shrine of St James the Great in Compostela
in northern Spain.

Staying the night

Travel was not easy, comfortable or safe. There
were few places where travelers could put up
for the night. Monasteries had a duty to
accommodate travelers, and if you were rich
enough you could stay at manor houses or
castles on the way. Others had to make do at
inns, which were not obviously dangerous.
Most people traveled on horseback, although
an elaborate cart, called a char, with a canvas
roof was available in Chaucer's time.

△ Here the Bayeux
tapestry shows one of
William the Conqueror's
specially built ships for
his invasion army of 1066.
In shape it is very similar
to Viking boats. It has no
oars but is driven by sail,
with a steering rudder at
the stern (back).

▽ Travelers in the early
16th century in Holland
arrive for May Day
celebrations on horseback,
on foot and by boat. The
river boat is paddled easily
by one person, while the
musicians play, and the
man on the prow fends off
the arches of the bridge.

▷ A medieval bridge at
Karitaina in southern
Greece, built by the Franks
in 1254 near their castle.
Notice the small chapel
with a cross on top
half-way across.

▽ This 15th-century
illustration from *The Book
of Marvels* shows travelers
from Europe outside the
walls of Peking. The artist
did not know what Peking
looked like and so had to
make up the view.

Moving goods

Merchants often had to move their goods over long distances. Wherever possible, water transport was used, as it had been since prehistoric times. It was cheaper and easier than road transport. Crusaders saw very different types of ships in the Mediterranean than those used in northern Europe.

Finding the way was much improved by medieval inventions – the compass and the astrolabe. The astrolabe was still used until the 18th century. Other maps, as we shall see on pages 74-75, were in use from the 14th and 15th centuries.

FRANCE

Most important changes in the government of France took place in the 13th century under King Louis IX. He became king in 1226 and reigned until his death in 1270. If you look again at the map of the Plantagenet Empire (page 29) you will see the differences which had taken place. The map here shows the later situation in France and Belgium in the 13th century. The dukes of Burgundy ruled the large territory that included the land still known as Burgundy today, though it never became a state.

The reign of Louis IX (St Louis)

Under previous kings of France the lands ruled directly by the king had been extended. Under Louis IX the kingdom did not grow. He wanted to put a stop to the violent way disputes were being settled and encourage people to use the law courts. The *parlement* was the main royal court of law. Some of the new territories were ruled by Louis' brothers; others were under the King of England's control. For six years Louis fought a crusade against the Muslims. He was once captured and had to be ransomed.

At home, during his reign, he encouraged education and the church. The first French universities were founded. In Paris there were many artists, masons and sculptors employed on new works. Paris became the most important center of book production of the time.

◁ This illustration from a 15th-century French manuscript shows the assassination of John the Fearless, Duke of Burgundy, in 1419 at Montereau.

△ Before machines were invented, farmers had to use flails to beat the seed from cornstalks. Here a 15th-century French book shows this happening at harvest in August.

Feet
6500
4275
1300
650
0

● Important settlement

Features located at a settlement
● Monastery
▲ Castle
■ University

—·—·— Boundary, 13th century

English Channel

Bruges
Ghent
St Omer
Tournai
Arras
Schelde
Somme
Arques
Corbie
Fécamp
Premontré
Aisne
Rethel
Rouen
Beauvais
Reims
Caen
Château Gaillard
Seine
St Clair
Pierrefonds
Coutances
Royaumont
Marne
Châlons
St Pol de Léon
St Evroult
Montfort
Paris
St Brieuc
Mt St Michel
Sées
Etampes
Seine
Quimper
Chartres
Troyes
Rennes
Les Clairets
Sens
Clairvaux
Vannes
Vilaine
Le Mans
Orléans
Fleury
Pontigny
Langres
Angers
Loire
Montereau
Flavigny
Nantes
Fontevrault
Tours
Amboise
Cher
Vézelay
Dijon
Loire
Loches
Beaulieu
Citeaux
Thouars
Chinon
FRANCE
Bourges
Nevers
Autun
St Maixent
Poitiers
La Ferté
La Rochelle
Charroux
Cluny
Saône
Charlieu
Vienne
Limoges
Saintes
Clermont-Ferrand
Angoulême
Ventadour
MASSIF
Périgueux
Brive-la-Gaillarde
Bordeaux
Dordogne
Aurillac
Le Puy
Castillon
CENTRAL
Allier
Villandraut
Garonne
Cahors
Lot
Mende
Bazas
Agen
Rodez
Moissac
Tarn
Adour
Albi
Uzès
Dax
La Couvertoirade
Nîmes
Bayonne
Auch
Toulouse
Lodève
Lescar
Montpellier
Lourdes
Montaner
Carcassonne
Aude
Narbonne
PYRENEES
St Betrand

Mediterranean Sea

Scale 1 : 4 000 000
0   100 km
0   80 miles

B   C   D

5

4

3

2

1

▷ The small village of Couvertoirade, in southern France, was on one of the routes pilgrims took on their journey to the shrine of St James the Great at Compostela in northern Spain. This village, built on a rock, was taken by the Templar Knights in 1182. The knights built a castle there in the early 13th century. The Order of Templars was set up to protect pilgrims to the Holy Lands and to shrines in other lands. When the order was dissolved in 1312, La Couvertoirade passed to another order of knights – the Hospitalers, who defended the sick. The wall and towers you can see today were built in 1439. It is a fine example of a heavily fortified village.

▽ An illustration from a French book about hunting, called *The Book of the Hunt*, written in the late 14th century by Gaston Fébus, Count of Foix. Here the hunters, in the middle of whom sits the Count himself, prepare for a boar hunt.

Medieval Paris

The modern capital city of Paris, France, takes its name from the Parisi tribe who lived in the area before the Romans invaded Gaul. The earliest occupation was on the largest of the islands in the River Seine which now flows through the city.

The medieval capital

From the 6th century onwards, Paris was gradually developed beyond the Roman walls and suburbs. Swamps around the River Seine were drained, monasteries built and the town became wealthy. The King of the Franks, Clovis, made Paris his capital in 508, and it became the permanent capital of France by the year 1000. The Cathedral of Notre-Dame (Our Lady) was completed in the 14th century.

Much of medieval Paris was destroyed during the reign of Louis XIV in the 17th century and later when Napoleon III built 60 new streets through the old town.

▷ Medieval Paris. The twin towers of the Cathedral of Notre-Dame dominate this view of the Île de la Cité, the island in the middle of the River Seine connected to the rest of the city by bridges. Barges brought goods to wharfs around the island, and houses and shops lined the wooden bridges.

▽ Paris during the 14th century. Nobles are attended by their servants in an illustration from Jean Froissart's accounts of life and war at the time. The city, crowded with houses and churches, is well protected by its wall, gates and towers.

ITALY

Until the middle of the 6th century Italy was still considered part of the Roman Empire. Then it was invaded by the Lombards in 568. It was unique in medieval Europe because the king of the Lombards was always a foreigner and after 774 had no authority over the whole of what we know as Italy today. In the 10th century it was under the control of the German rulers. Some of the northern cities – such as Venice, Milan and Florence – remained independent.

Five major powers

The powerful kings of Aragon, based in Catalonia in northeast Spain, gradually acquired more and more territory to include the Balearic Islands and then the islands further east. In the 15th century they also took over the Kingdom of Naples.

By the early 15th century there were five major powers in Italy. The north was divided between the Duchy of Milan and the Venetian Republic. To the south the Republic of Florence was the strongest state in Tuscany. In the center lay the Papal State (of Rome, ruled by the pope) and further south the Kingdom of Naples.

Powerful families and republics

In many territories power was held by committees of people elected to office – republics. This gradually changed as one powerful man, or family, emerged. For example, the Visconti family held Milan; the Medici took over the Republic of Florence; and Venice was ruled by a head of state, a *doge*, who was elected for life.

Condottieri (mercenaries)

Towns, republics, duchies and kingdoms were often at war. Local troops, called the militia, protected most towns until the 14th century. A change then took place as towns bought the service of mercenary soldiers, called *condottieri*. They were often difficult to get rid of after the war, and towns were forced to continue paying for them – a sort of blackmail. One such mercenary was Bartolomeo Colleoni, captain-general of the army of Venice. Colleoni died a very rich man in 1476.

▽ This map of Rome was made in 1323 by Paolo di Venezia. It shows some of the monuments that would interest travelers, such as the walls of the city.

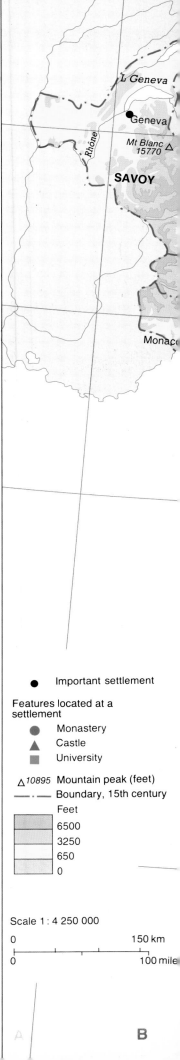

● Important settlement

Features located at a settlement

● Monastery

▲ Castle

■ University

△10895 Mountain peak (feet)

–·– Boundary, 15th century

Feet

6500
3250
650
0

Scale 1 : 4 250 000

0   150 km

0   100 mile

San Gimignano

Today some of the most impressive sights in Tuscany in northern Italy are the medieval fortified towns perched on hilltops. San Gimignano is one of these, with strongly built and easily defended towers. In 12th-century Italy there were many towns such as this that were independent and controlled the lands around. Each town needed strong defenses to fight off others that might claim its territory.

Rule by the people

By the 13th century the "people" – the *popolo* – began to take over control of towns from the wealthy and powerful nobles who had run them before. The sort of people who now governed the towns were lawyers, merchants and guilds of important industries, such as cloth manufacture. San Gimignano was like one great castle with a wall and towers protecting the limits of the town. Also important in the town at this time was the *palazzo* – the residence of the town's government.

△ The Palazzo del Popolo was built in the 13th century as the headquarters of the town's chief magistrate.

▽ San Gimignano once had 72 towers like these. The land around was known for its wine and grain production and was a center for the spice saffron.

Florence

Florence is unlike many other towns in Tuscany because it is built on a flat plain. Its position is important, as it is built on both sides of the River Arno. The river was used for defense, trade and communication.

Florence in the 13th century

Florence became very important in the 13th century because of the industries it developed. The town was famous for its cloth making, and the products were exported not only to other towns in Italy but also to France. By the late 13th century the town was governed by committees made up from members of its most powerful guilds, or associations, of professions and industries. The wealth created by these industries helped pay for the building of a wall to enclose the town, begun in about 1290.

Government by the few

The richer men who lent money to the city government in the 14th century eventually

▽ At the narrowest point of the River Arno is the Ponte Vecchio. A bridge has been here since the 10th century. This one, lined with shops, was rebuilt in 1345. It replaced one that was swept away in floods during 1333. Shops built along the side of the river emphasize the commercial importance of the river in Florence.

took control of the city's affairs. Only in the 15th century did one family, the Medici, become the ruling family. Florence, already wealthy, began to conquer other major towns around, such as Arezzo in 1385 and Pisa in 1406.

The buildings of Florence

Florence was just as famous for its art and architecture as it was for its trade and industries. The wealth created from its industries paid for many of the fine buildings, such as the Palazzo Vecchio, which we can still see today.

It was not only architects who found employment in Florence. The town had many other artists, sculptors, masons, glaziers, painters and goldsmiths. They helped decorate the many churches and public buildings of the city.

Schools and a university

The towns of Tuscany, Florence in particular, were well known for their schools. Standards of literacy were high, and the great Italian poet Dante (1265-1321), who wrote the *Divine Comedy*, was a Florentine. But for training in law and in medicine it was necessary to go to the greater universities, such as Bologna. In Florence, from the late 14th and 15th centuries, some of the leading citizens encouraged the rediscovery of Greek classics and their study.

▽ Towering above the medieval buildings of Florence is its *duomo* – cathedral – which was begun in 1296 but not consecrated as a cathedral until 1436. It is called Santa Maria del Fiore (Saint Mary of the Flower). Two parts of the cathedral stand out above the main body of the church. The great cupola or dome was begun in 1420, and the campanile (bell-tower) covered in marble was finished in 1387.

Genoa

The trading town of Genoa had one very important advantage over some of its rivals – a good natural harbor. It had new markets opened to it with the success of the First Crusade in the 11th century. The wealth from its trade allowed the town to grow and develop both its harbor and its defenses.

International trade

Genoa's position on the northwest coast of Italy meant that trade links were developed

▽ The Porta Soprana, with its two towers, is part of the city wall built around Genoa in 1155.

especially with western Europe and Africa. Cloth was the most important import from other towns in Italy and from Germany and Spain. In return, Genoa traded dyes from the East, spices, perfumes and precious stones. Genoa established trading posts in Africa as bases for its merchants.

Trading rivalries

Genoa's nearest rival was Pisa. In 1284 Genoa defeated Pisa in battle and gained control of the town's trade links. Its other rival, Venice, was more difficult to beat. Venice had set up its trade links in the East very early on and had a monopoly in Constantinople. Genoa founded posts in Asia Minor (now Turkey) to import alum, which was needed to fix dyes in cloth.

TRADE

Few communities can exist simply on what they can produce themselves. People usually have to import goods – extra food, clothes and equipment, for example – from elsewhere. Goods might have to be brought from the next village or a nearby town. But some items have to be carried vast distances. In medieval times, areas and towns came to specialize in particular goods, such as the woollen industry in Flanders. Most important towns grew as trading centers rather than as places where goods were made.

Protecting the trade routes

Those who traded – the merchants – had to arrange for their own goods to be fetched and protected. There were many dangers. For example, piracy was a real problem in northern Europe in the 13th century. There was no overall law to protect all Europe as there had been in the Roman period.

The great center of trade in the medieval period was the Mediterranean. The Crusades made it possible for pilgrims and merchants to travel to the East and so helped trade develop.

▽ European trade in the 14th century. Most trade was carried out by sea. Not all overland routes are shown, but notice how many make use of rivers – to Paris and Toledo for example. Some areas developed their natural resources for trade (such as wine or metals), while others became centers for particular trades (cloth making, for example).

Land routes and sea routes

Great fairs were held all over Europe to exchange goods. At first most trade was carried out by merchants using pack animals. This meant slow journeys with the threat of attacks by robbers. It also meant that only small quantities of goods could be carried. By the 14th century ships were increasingly used for trade. Large quantities of goods, such as grain for bread, could be shipped from, say, Sicily to feed the townspeople of Bruges or Antwerp.

Trading nations

Important items of trade included cloth, timber and some foodstuffs such as grain and wine. Two Italian towns in particular established themselves as great centers of trade. Genoa was well placed to trade both inland to northern Europe and by sea in the western and eastern Mediterranean. And the government in Venice was able to use its harbors to establish many trade routes.

Throughout the eastern Mediterranean you can still see Venetian forts that helped protect their trade routes. There are many on mainland Greece and its islands, in particular on Crete.

◁ Guilds (or associations) of trades and crafts were common from the 13th century. Members of the guild of cloth merchants in Bologna, Italy, are shown here filling a street with their stalls and booths.

▽ Genoa, Italy, was one of the earliest cities known for its money changers or bankers from the 12th century. Here the bankers are counting coins to give to the town's widows and orphans.

THE BRITISH ISLES

Many of the fields and roads that can be seen in Britain today were well established long before the Romans conquered the country in 43. Since then many different peoples have made changes to the map of Britain. The names of places, for example, can often be traced to the later invasions of Anglo-Saxon, Viking or Norman settlers.

English boundaries established

By the 13th century England was a kingdom and could properly be called one country. It was no longer as closely linked to France as it had been before. The king had established a *parliament* to advise him. The king sent for powerful people to represent different parts of the country. They came from the shires (for example, Oxfordshire or Yorkshire) and from important towns (such as Rochester). Smaller units in the country, the ecclesiastical parishes, had been established before the Norman invasion and continued to run local affairs.

Royal and church lands and ports

Even at this time some lands remained totally in the hands of either the king or the church, as the map shows. Five south-coast ports, called the Cinque Ports (*cinq* is French for "five"), had special privileges and duties. They provided ships for the navy in return for tax allowances.

Wales and the king

The situation in Wales was different. No one prince was strong enough to dominate the whole country. When the princes of Gwynedd in the north tried to do this they were stopped by an alliance between King Edward I of England and some of the other Welsh princes. After 1284 King Edward took over the government of Gwynedd himself and built a number of castles there.

Ireland

Although King Henry II claimed the lordship of Ireland and many Norman lords were established there, the English never gained control of the whole of the island. By 1485 the English really controlled only an area known as the Pale around Dublin. The boundaries of medieval Ireland underwent significant changes in more recent times.

◁ One of the best places to see what an English medieval town was like is York in the north of the country. This is the area known as the Shambles where wooden buildings overhang the street to gain as much floor space as possible. Most of the buildings have now been restored.

▽ Ireland has been a Christian country since the 5th century. Christian crosses, like this one at Castledermot, were built in many places. This is one of 50 that still survive from before the 9th century. It is highly carved and shows the suffering of Christ.

◁ The Angel Choir inside the cathedral at Lincoln, a town of about 4,000 people in the Norman period. The cathedral was begun in the late 11th century. The Normans built four cathedrals, which were served by canons (see pages 42-43). There were already nine in Britain during the Saxon period. Lincoln Cathedral was gradually enlarged and completed in the late 14th century.

Settlements
◆ Cinque port
● Important town

Features located at a settlement
● Monastery
▲ Castle
■ University

—··— Boundary, 13th century
——— Pale boundary

Feet
1625
650
0

Scale 1 : 4 000 000
0 _____ 100 km
0 _____ 80 miles

Orkney Islands

Outer Hebrides

The Minch

Dunskeath
Dunvegan
Inverness
Nairn
Banff
Skye
Eileen Donan
Spey
GRAMPIAN MTS
Dee
Aberdeen
Inner Hebrides
Inverey
SCOTLAND
Forfar
North Sea
Mull
Tay
Perth
Iona
Abernethy
Stirling
North Berwick
Islay
Tarbert
Paisley
Rutherglen
Edinburgh
Berwick
Tweed
Roxburgh
Ayr
Clyde
Alnwick
Dunaverty
Holywood
Hermitage
Tyne
Newcastle
Wigtown
Carlisle
Durham
Londonderry
Appleby
IRELAND
Carrickfergus
Mourne
Lough Neagh
Inch
Richmond
Scarborough
Assaroe
PENNINES
Armagh
Killala
Isle of Man
Lancaster
York
Boyle
Dundalk
Roscommon
PALE
Trim
Clitheroe
L Corrib
Athlone
Dublin
Irish Sea
ENGLAND
Galway
Shannon
Barrow
Lincoln
Beaumaris
Gonway
Chester
Tattershall
Suir
Castledermot
Caernarvon
Newcastle-under-Lyme
Limerick
Kilkenny
Harlech
Nottingham
Norwich
Ardfert
Clonmel
Bere
Trent
Blackwater
Shrewsbury
Peterborough
Waterford
CAMBRIAN MTS
Bridgnorth
Nene
Bury St Edmunds
Cork
WALES
Warwick
Cambridge
Severn
Hereford
Bedford
Colchester
St David's
Gloucester
Oxford
St Albans
Dynevor
Thames
London
Pembroke
Windsor
Rochester
Sandwich
Llandaff
Canterbury
Dover
Devizes
Hythe
Romney
Glastonbury
Salisbury
Winchester
Arundel
Hastings
Exe
Porchester
Exeter
Corfe
Truro
English Channel

North Sea

North Channel

St George's Channel

CASTLES

The word for a castle in medieval Latin was *castrum* or *castellum*. "Castle" is often used for any fortified place; the Latin word was used by the Romans for a military fort. Other, later peoples made fortifications, of course. The Saxons, for example, fortified their towns against the Danes and called them *burhs*. There is a *burh* at Dover, on the southern coast of Britain, but castles of later periods have been built on top of it.

Built by the powerful

A castle was a safe place. It had to be secure against attack and a last resort for the regular inhabitants and often the people who lived around it. The site of a castle had to be carefully chosen. The best places were often already defended simply by the landscape – on a high ridge or with sheer cliffs on one side, for example. To build a castle you had to be powerful and you had to be rich.

The king often built a number of castles to hold power over the land. The king could not control all his territory alone. He gave some land away to those he could trust. In France the king granted lands and the right to control them. These were called fiefs. In return the barons or the knights gave the king their loyalty and supplied him with fighting men.

Castles of timber and earth

In some parts of Europe the first castles built in the 10th century were made of timber (for walls, gates and buildings inside) and earth (for the outer defenses, for example). In 11th-century England they were called motte-and-bailey castles.

A great mound (motte) of earth was constructed and a wooden building put on top. This was the keep or strongest point in the castle. Around it was the bailey – an area surrounded by walls of earth and timber – where the people lived. Some castles had an inner bailey (around the keep) and an outer bailey, also protected by a wall and guard towers.

Building in stone

In England after 1150 very few timber and earth castles were built. Stone could provide a much stronger and more permanent building. This type of building was very expensive though.

The stone castle at Dover built in the late 12th century cost about £7,000. This was a huge sum of money in those times. Building in stone allowed the architects to develop better ideas for making the castle a safe place to live in.

Castles were built to protect the interests of a particular lord or king or to provide a garrison for soldiers. But they were also for living in. The castle was the fortified home not only for the knight but also for his family, his servants, his craftspeople and his fighting men. In times of trouble the bailey courtyard, already full of buildings and animals, became the temporary home of villagers around.

◁ Curemonte Castle in Brive la Gaillarde in France is actually two castles joined by a surrounding wall with round towers built in the 14th century.

▽ Reconstruction drawing of the motte at Abinger, Surrey, in England. The mound, built by the Normans in the 11th century, had a timber watchtower on top.

▽ The castle at Frangocastello, Crete, built by the Venetians to protect their trade routes in 1371.

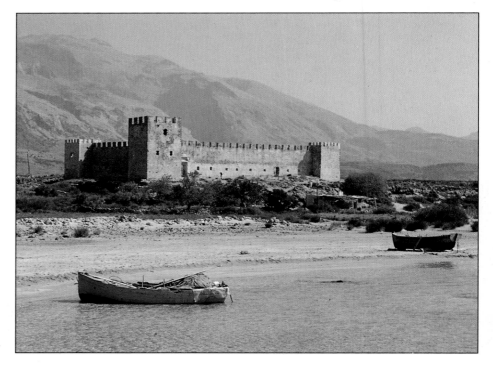

△ The Normans first built a castle at Rochester in Kent soon after the Battle of Hastings in 1066. A motte-and-bailey castle defended the crossing of the River Medway. The later stone castle on the same site, and the great cathedral, as above, were begun by Bishop Gundulf in about 1087.

▷ The keep of Rochester Castle is one of the largest in England. This huge building, with its three floors and roof battlements, was begun in 1127. There are no doors at ground level – attackers had to get past the guard tower and portcullis. On various floors there are bedrooms, halls for eating in, lavatories and a chapel. A well inside the keep provided fresh water.

THE COUNTRYSIDE

Today in Europe most people go to the supermarket for their daily food. Some of that food may come from the land around the town or village, but most will come from further away, from foreign countries. Medieval people living in the countryside ate only what they produced on their own land.

In most European countries medieval kings claimed control over the land but allowed trusted lords the rights to much of it. The lords of estates relied on tenants to work the land and collected either rents or produce each year.

Using all the land's resources

The amount of land an ordinary family was able to work varied from country to country and from place to place. In England a family with about 12 hectares (30 acres) to plow could probably live quite well from what food they could produce. Other families had to make do with half of that.

Besides growing their crops, people had the right to graze their animals on meadows and rough land. Most people had a few animals such as sheep, pigs and chickens and an ox or a horse for plowing. People also had the right to collect other things from the land – turf for roofing and to burn, wood, nuts and berries, and bracken for beds and for animal food.

Hunting and fishing

For country people trying to live off the land, the right to fish, catch eels and frogs or net birds

was essential. In some parts of Europe hunting animals in forests provided a ready source of food. Fish was an important part of the medieval diet. Monasteries, castles and manor houses usually had their own ponds to ensure a regular supply of fresh fish.

For the wealthy, hunting was a sport to enjoy and an important way to keep healthy and in good shape for warfare. Hunting areas were protected and guarded, both from scavenging animals and from those without the right to hunt. There were inhumane penalties for any people who were caught poaching.

◁ Hunting with falcons was a popular sport for the well-born. Notice that the handlers are wearing strong leather gauntlets. The illustration comes from a book on the subject of falconry made in the mid-13th century for Manfred, King of Sicily.

▷ This illustration from a French book was made about 1411 to illustrate the month of March. Pictures like this add to our evidence about life in the countryside gathered from archaeological work and from documents. The fields are small, and the man in the foreground is plowing with two oxen. Fields were often divided into strips and the strips allotted to the villagers so that each family had some good and some poor land to work. In the field further back, workers are pruning vines for the wine harvest.

◁ Refreshment was not forgotten after a day's hunting – notice the dogs, horses and hunting horns. This illustration and the one on the right are from *The Book of the Hunt* by Gaston Fébus written in 1387 in France.

▷ Gaston Fébus was an expert on hunting stag and boar using dogs. He also used nets, for trapping hares and foxes. Nets of rope are being made here. Much finer nets were used for catching all types of birds – from songbirds to pigeons.

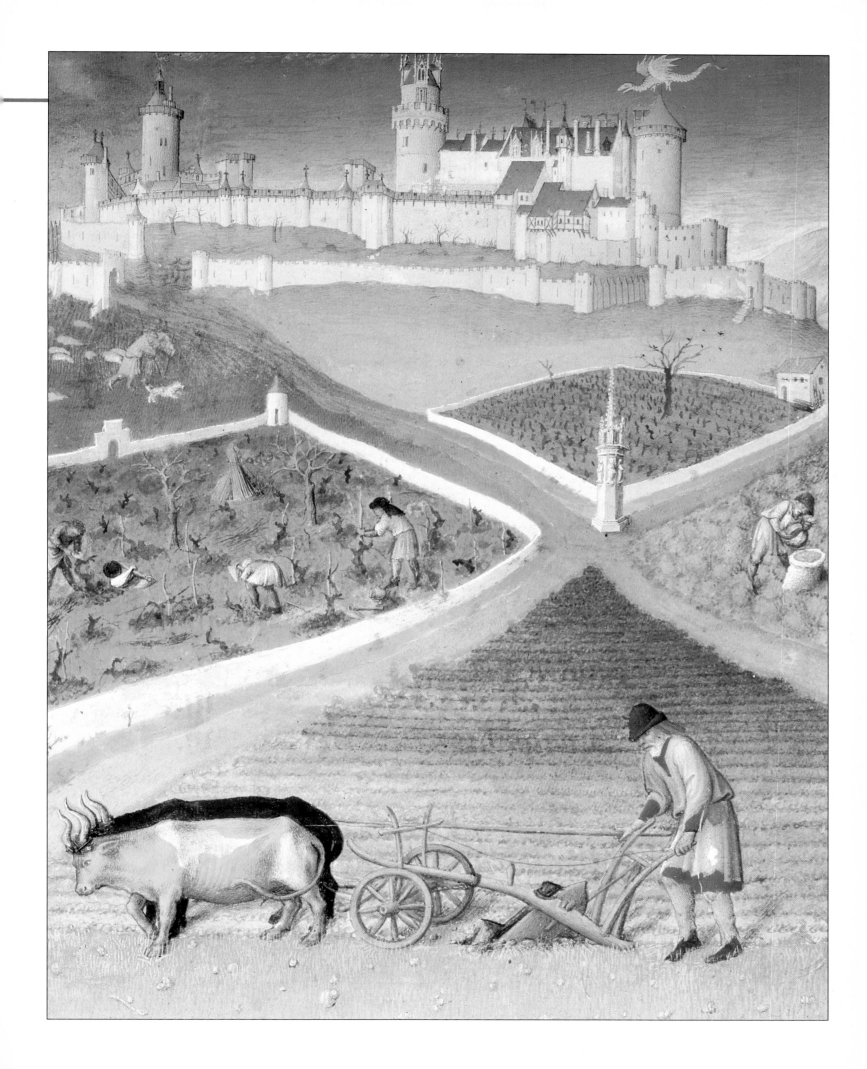

SPAIN AND PORTUGAL

Part of the story of medieval Europe is the struggle between two great religious faiths – Christianity and Islam. Much of this struggle took place in the area later known as Spain and Portugal.

An Islamic Mediterranean

At the time of the death of the Islamic prophet Muhammad in 632, the Muslims controlled the area of Arabia on the eastern side of the Red Sea. Throughout the 7th century they moved north into the Holy Land and east along the Persian Gulf and Arabian Sea. They also conquered north Africa, reaching Ceuta (near Gibraltar) in 709. From here they struck out into Europe. By 750 the Muslims occupied Portugal, most of Spain and part of southern France.

The Christians gain control

Although the Christians held a small amount of territory in the north of Spain, it was not until the middle of the 11th century that they had much success against Muslim occupation. They called this fight the *Reconquista*, or reconquest. Most reconquest took place either in the late 11th century or in the early part of the 13th century. Land was taken away from the Muslims and given to the new conquerors, but Muslims were allowed to live in the new kingdoms, at least until the 16th century.

Settlements
◆ Christian center
● Important town

Features located at a settlement
● Monastery
▲ Castle
■ University

—·— Boundary, 14th century

▽ The town of Avila in the kingdom of Castile, now Spain. Its impressive town walls were put up after the town had been reconquered from the Muslims in the late 11th century. The walls are 40 feet high, defended by huge round towers and eight gates. The town had originally been founded by the Romans, and a lot of Roman buildings were reused to make the fortifications.

Bay of Biscay

CANTABRIAN MOUNTAINS

PYRENEES

NAVARRE

CASTILE

ARAGON

SIERRA DE GUADARRAMA

SERRANIA DE CUENCA

GRANADA

SIERRA NEVADA

Santander
Covadonga
San Sebastian
viedo
León
Pamplona
Leyre
Sahagún
Huelgas
Burgos
Calahorra
San Juan de la Peña
Alquézar
Huesca
Ripoll
Besalú
Gerona
Palencia
Arlaniza
Fitero
Soria
Tarazona
Saragossa
Lérida
Montserrat
Barcelona
Zamora
Valladolid
Peñafiel
Osma
Caspe
Poblet
Santa Creus
Tarragona
na del Campo
Coca
Piedra
Salamanca
Segovia
Tortosa
Avila
Albarracín
Madrid
Alcalá
CASTILE
S Geronimo de Yuste
Agal
Cuenca
Segorbe
Toledo
Guadalupe
Alcázar de San Juan
Valencia
Ciudad Real
Chinchilla
San Martin
Alicante
Baños de la Encina
Baeza
Murcia
Córdoba
Jaén
Cartagena
alá de Guadaira
Santafé
Granada
Almería
Málaga
Gibraltar

Ebro
Valderaduey
Duero
Jalón
Tagus
Guadiana
Júcar
Turia
Segura
Guadalquivir
Genil
Cinca
Ebro

△ The northern town of Alquézar was founded by the Muslims but captured by the Spanish in 1087.

Ciudadela
Minorca
Palma
Balearic Islands
Majorca

Feet
6500
3250
650
0

Scale 1 : 3 400 000

0   150 km

0   100 miles

73

C   D   E

MAPMAKING

The earliest maps we know of in the world were made by the Sumerians in the Near East in about 3200 BC. The Greeks also made maps, and it was to these that the first medieval mapmakers referred.

Ptolemy – Greek mapmaker

Ptolemy, who was from the Greek city of Alexandria in Egypt, wrote his work *Geography* in the 2nd century. Copies were made in the 13th century, and the book was translated into Latin in 1406.

▽ "EVROPA MVNDI PARS QVARTA" – "Europe a quarter of the world." Part of a book written in Latin in about 1120, called *Liber Floridus*. The author thought that the world was divided into four quarters of a circle.

Sea charts and atlases

Ptolemy's work, together with specially drawn maps, was printed in Italy in 1477. But there had been new detailed maps in Europe before that, in the 13th century, used mainly as a help for navigation at sea. The magnetic compass had been known as an aid since the late 12th century. These sea charts, the compass and the astrolabe (see page 48) required a knowledge of mathematics to work out the right course. The earliest atlas that survives today was made for King Charles V of France in 1375.

△ A picture map of Inglemoor, England, made in 1405. It has been drawn with points of the compass, rivers, bridges, villages, fields and the moor itself in the center. It was produced for a court hearing when ownership of the land was disputed.

Specialized maps

Specialized maps and charts were produced in the 14th century for traders from centers such as Venice and Genoa. The Mediterranean world was very well mapped. For example, in 1320 Marino Sanudo, from Venice, wrote about the problem of conquering the Holy Land from the Muslims and sent his book to the Pope with a set of maps made by Pietro Visconte.

Maps of the world

In the 15th century the invention of printing meant that maps could easily be produced from woodcuts or from copper plates. It was in this century that voyages of discovery were made and new maps of the wider world had to be produced. The Portuguese were the first people in Europe to set sail for new lands across seas that had never been charted before.

▽ This sea chart of part of western Europe was made in 1497 by Freducci d'Ancona. Each country is easily recognizable today, and the coastlines have been accurately plotted. Compare this map with the modern one of Europe on page 8. Notice here that the interior of the countries is not plotted in detail – for example, Paris and London are not shown.

◁ Cartographers (map- and chart-makers) at work on a coastline from their ship. The west coast of Africa was plotted by a cartographer from Venice in 1448, but the Portuguese captains sent out by Prince Henry the Navigator had reached this coast 17 years before.

JOURNEY TO COMPOSTELA

Pilgrimages were very popular in medieval Europe. People so treasured the remains and possessions of the many saints that they believed they could be healed by them. Pilgrims also made their long journeys in the hope that their sins would be forgiven.

Dangerous journeys

Many pilgrims probably thought that the danger of long-distance travel was punishment enough for their sins. Jerusalem was one place that was much visited, but when the Muslims conquered the city in 638 other shrines became popular. From the 11th century parties of pilgrims were organized, such as the one described in Chaucer's *Canterbury Tales*.

The shrine of St James

The more important shrines were those of the Apostles of Christ. People believed the tomb discovered in about 830 at Compostela in northern Spain was that of St James the Apostle. A church was built there, and pilgrims from Spain began making the journey. The news of the shrine soon spread. At the end of the 11th century the Pope ordered the bishop of the region Iria to move his headquarters there.

There were four main pilgrim routes from France to Compostela, though people also came there from further away. Along the routes monasteries were built, and villages and towns became wealthy from the pilgrim trade.

▷ Three of the main pilgrim routes across France came together at Ostabat. In medieval times it was prosperous and catered for large numbers of travelers. Now Ostabat is a quiet village.

▷ This church at Conques, France, was built in the mid-11th century on the route from Le Puy to Ostabat. At Conques a local child saint was revered – St Foy.

▽ At Santillana, on the northern coast of Spain, this church was built in the Romanesque style. This style of architecture was popular in the late 11th and 12th centuries and copied ideas from Rome.

Paris

Seine

Marne

Chartres

Yonne

Orléans

Auxerre

Tours

Loire

Vézelay

Bourges

Nevers

Poitiers

Allier

Loire

St Jean-d'Angély

Aulnay

Limoges

St Léonard-de-Noblat

Clermont-Ferrand

Saintes

FRANCE

Périgueux

Le Puy

Blaye

Bergerac

Dordogne

Aurillac

Rocamadour

Bordeaux

Garonne

Conques

Belin

Lot

Cahors

Rhône

Bay of Biscay

Agen

Moissac

St Sever

Adour

Aire

Auch

Toulouse

Nîmes

Arles

Montpellier

St Gilles

Aix

Santillana

Santander

Sorde

Ostabat

San Sebastián

Guernica

Valcarlos

St Jean-Pied-de-Port

SPAIN

Cize Pass

Roncesvalles

Somport Pass

PYRENEES

Mediterranean Sea

Pamplona

Monreal

Canfranc

Santo Domingo de la Calzada

Puente de la Reina

Aragon

Jaca

Sahagun

Los Arcos

Sanguesa

Carrion

Tardajos

Burgos

Villafranca

Logroño

Najera

romista

Castrogeriz

Huesca

Palencia

Ebro

Monastery

Town or village visited by pilgrims

Mountain pass

Land over 3250 feet

Approximate route taken by pilgrims

Scale 1 : 3 500 000

0 _____ 100km

0 _____ 75 miles

△ Legends about St James arose late in the medieval period. They were probably based less on fact than on people's need to believe in miracles and wonders.

SWITZERLAND, GERMANY AND THE LOW COUNTRIES

Some parts of medieval Europe developed quite separate histories, which were not connected with the establishment of the large Roman Empire. However, the German Empire or Holy Roman Empire looked back to Rome and tried to reestablish some of its traditions.

Development of an empire

"The Empire," as it was known, was not completely controlled by one emperor. The 14th century was a period of great change in medieval Europe and in the German Empire a number of families held power. Two families in particular ruled this empire: the Luxembourg family from 1346 to 1437 and then the Hapsburgs from 1438 onwards. However, a number of separate states and cities that declared themselves "free" also made up the empire.

Governing a large territory

Some noble families claimed the throne of the empire, and wars frequently went on between powerful groups. However, the emperor had to be elected by princes and had to influence them and the independent cities and states in order to remain in overall control.

Switzerland

This area in particular shows the complicated way in which the empire was formed and governed. Switzerland had been part of the territory of the German Empire since the 11th century and was ruled by a number of noble families. In 1291 a confederation of independent districts and prosperous towns joined together. This showed itself to be powerful and not afraid to use its army to resist the German princes. Switzerland was nevertheless part of the German Empire.

The Low Countries

Another example of the complicated nature of the empire can be seen in the countries which bordered the North Sea. Flanders had been part of the French kingdom but passed into the territory of the dukes of Burgundy, who also took over Brabant in 1404. In fact by the middle part of the 15th century the dukes of Burgundy had become very rich and powerful. They held land from the Swiss border north to Holland and built up Antwerp as a trading port.

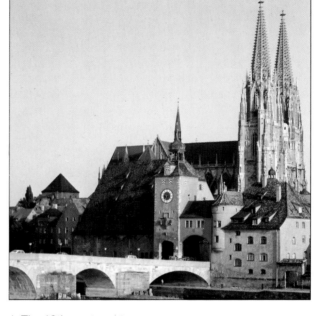

△ The 12th-century stone bridge across the Danube at the cathedral city of Regensburg, Germany.

▷ Toplerschlösschen im Rosenthal. This fortified German tower guards the town's mills.

▽ Rothenburg and its town walls were rebuilt in the 14th century.

North Sea

● Boulogne

● Amiens

Auxe

Loire

Nevers ●

Settlements

■ Hanse town (see also pages 88–89)

○ Independent city

● Important town

Features located at a settlement

● Monastery

▲ Castle

■ University

△15770 Mountain peak (feet)

— ⋅ — Boundary, 14th–15th centuries

Feet

6500
3250
650
0
Below sea level

Scale 1 : 5 500 000

0 ——— 150 km

0 ——— 100 miles

A

Baltic Sea

■ Kiel

■ Rostock
◉ Greifswald

◉ Ritzebüttel
◉ Lübeck
◉ Hamburg
Stettin ■

■ Groningen
Oldenburg ●
● Bremen
Elbe
● Havelberg

Deventer
● Utrecht
■ Osnabrück
● Hanover
● Brandenburg
Frankfurt ■

Münster ●
Herford ●
◉ Goslar
Quedlinburg ●
Luban ●
Breslau ■

● Antwerp
◉ Dortmund
Weser
Leipzig ●
Meissen ●

Brussels ●
● Louvain
Essen ●
GERMAN   EMPIRE
Erfurt ◉
Zeitz ●

■ Cologne
● Marburg
SUDENTEN MTS

◉ Aix
Fulda ●
Königingrätz ●

Stablo ●
● Koblenz
Schweinfurt ◉
Waldsassen ●
Prague ■

Cambrai
ARDENNES
◉ Frankfurt
Olomouc ●

Trier ●
Heidelberg ●
Würzburg ●
BOHEMIAN
Vltava

Rethel ●
Luxembourg ●
Toplerschlösschen im Rosenthal
Brünn ●

◉ Metz
Trifels ▲
Speyer ◉
Rothenburg ◉
Regensburg ◉
FOREST
Budweis ●

Bar ●
Strasbourg ●
Gmünd ◉
Nördlingen ◉
Ingolstadt ■

VOSGES MTS
Tübingen ●
Augsburg ●
Passau ●
Danube
Vienna ●

Münster ◉
BLACK
Alpirsbach ■
● Munich
Waidhofen ●

Luxeuil ●
FOREST
Danube
Buchau ◉
Salzburg ●

Basle ◉
Rhine
Constance ●
Lindau ●

Beaune ●
Besançon ◉
Zurich ◉
Innsbruck ●
Grossglockner △ 12453
Mur
Gurk ●

JURA MTS
Berne ●
Chur ●
Brixen ●
DOLOMITES
Drava

Mâcon
Lausanne ●
Disentis ◉
ALPS

L Geneva
Sierre ●
L Maggiore
Trent ●
Gorizia ●
Sava

Geneva ●
Mt Blanc 15770 △
Matterhorn 14682 △
L di Como

Aosta
Como ●
L di Garda
Vicenza ●

Milan ●

Turin ●
Piacenza ●
Po

Modena ●
Adriatic Sea

Genoa ●
APENNINES

Arles ●
Arno
Florence ●

Aix ■
Monaco ●
Ligurian Sea
Pisa ●
Siena ●

Mediterranean Sea

EVERYDAY LIFE

For very many people in medieval Europe life was hard – perhaps harder for those living in towns than for those in the countryside. Despite much poverty and disease, the population rose quickly. We think that there were about 22½ million inhabitants of western Europe in 950. By the middle of the 14th century this number had doubled.

Towns

Although most people lived in the country, more towns grew up in the medieval period. By our standards now they were not very big. The larger towns, such as Hamburg and London, each had between some 20,000 and 40,000 inhabitants by the 14th century. There were more than 100,000 people in only a very few cities, such as Paris, Milan and Venice. Town and countryside were not separated in quite the way they are today. Many townspeople cultivated gardens and fields and kept animals inside the town's walls.

Evidence about everyday life

While we have some evidence about the lives of ordinary people from documents and pictures, we can also find out a great deal from the results of archaeological work. For example, we can look at leather shoes preserved by being thrown into a well when they were worn out. Everyone in the medieval world used pottery – to store things in, to cook with and to eat from. Pottery fragments survive very well.

Industry

Industry was usually carried out in towns. Specialized workshops (not factories) were established, often in the place where the raw material was to be found. For example, we know that there was pottery production in Cologne in Germany by at least the 8th century. Much of the work was done by hand. Craftsmen carved animal bone and horn into everyday objects such as counters for games, combs, buttons and even ice skates. But machines were introduced where possible, to help with production. Spinning wheels and clocks were both medieval inventions. In the countryside wind- and watermills provided power. Watermills were used for sawing wood, making cloth and making paper, for example.

△ Wooden carving from the church at Fairford, England, showing a husband being battered by his wife. It is on a misericord, or "mercy seat." These are ledges cut under the tip-up seats to allow the clergy to take the weight off their feet during long church services. Many have humorous carvings.

◁ Inside a German kitchen the housewife or housekeeper (notice the bunch of keys) cooks over a wood fire. In the iron cauldron is the daily pottage, or soup-stew, made from vegetables and meat.

▽▷ Guilds often paid for stained-glass windows in churches (right). A drapers' (cloth makers') guild had these made showing carding (combing) the cloth and cutting the nap (the rough surface).

There were many small industries in towns, places for shops and where goods could be traded (below). This scene is of a German town in the early 16th century.

Guilds

Often, groups of specialized workers formed themselves into guilds – made up from masters who ran the shops of workmen. Each laid down rules for the way they worked, traded and trained new workers (the apprentices). Guild rules always stressed the importance of the members' religious duties. Like similar associations today, they also looked after their members and their members' families in times of trouble or hardship. Guilds played an important part in the running and government of some towns and could be very powerful.

BOHEMIA, HUNGARY, GREECE AND THE BALKANS

The area covered in the map on the right is vast—roughly eleven times the size of England. The history of this area in the medieval period is the most complicated in Europe. There were two main aspects to this history. One was the continuing involvement in this area of western European kings, states and cities. The other was the gradual increase in the size of the Muslim Empire under the Ottoman Turks.

The Ottoman threat

The Ottoman Turks, at the beginning of the 14th century, held only a small amount of land on the southern edge of the Black Sea. Through the 14th and 15th centuries they were able to gain control of Asia Minor, Greece and part of the Balkans. They took Constantinople, the capital of the Eastern Empire, in 1453. These Muslim Turks were dedicated soldiers. Their huge and effective armies had little difficulty in overcoming the divided forces of the western European princes who opposed them.

Greece and the Balkans

There were many groups in this area to fight the Muslim advance, but often they fought each other as well. The Order of the Knights of St John defended the island of Rhodes against the Muslims. The Venetians and the Genoese held territory in Greece and Asia Minor. Their occupation held back the Muslims, but these two cities were more interested in trade than in establishing a new Christian empire in the East. For much of the 14th century, in fact, they fought each other.

Other western groups were interested in this part of the world, but their military power was limited. The King of Aragon acquired Sicily in 1282, and then in the 14th century Catalans took Athens and a large area around it. For a time the French controlled some lands in Greece and northwards as far as Hungary. The situation changed often.

Bohemia

To the north of the area fought over by Muslims and Christians was the powerful kingdom of Bohemia. The Czechs, its most influential people, were ruled by their own kings until the 14th century. By then the king of Bohemia held the most important position in central Europe.

◁ The finely decorated west front of the abbey at Ják in western Hungary. This is 13th-century architecture, dating from the rebuilding of the abbey after the invasion of the Mongol hordes in 1241.

Bohemia took over a number of neighboring states, including Hungary and Lausitz. The ruler of the German Empire was elected by the king of Bohemia and six German princes. The first university of the German Empire was founded in Prague in 1348. At one time in the early 14th century the kings of Bohemia even ruled Poland.

▽ The castle and defensive walls of the Knights of St John on the island of Rhodes. The knights, driven out from Acre in the Holy Land, crusaded against the Muslims from Rhodes from 1310 to 1522.

Luckau
LAUSITZ
Glogow
Luban
Breslau
Elbe **Oder**
SUDENTEN
Eger
Prague Konigingratz
Racibórz
MTS
BOHEMIA
Klatovy **Iglau**
Olomouc
Vltava
Budweis
Zilina
Saros
Bratislava
Nitra
Lelesz
Danube
Esztergom **Ofen** **Eger**
Szatmar
Ják
HUNGARIAN **Oradea**
L Balaton
HUNGARY **Cluj**
Kalocsa
PLAIN
Pécs
Csanad
Drava _Mures_
Zagreb **Gyulafehervar**
Sava
Djakovo
Senj _TRANSYLVANIAN ALPS_
Dubica
DALMATIA **Belgrade** **Armenis** **WALLACHIA**
Zadar DINARIC **Tumu Severin**
Srebrenica Morava
Sibenik Sarajevo **Vidin** **Bucharest**
ALPS **Split** Danube **Silistria**
BOSNIA **Nis**
Durmitor △ **Nicopolis** **Varna**
8269 **Novi Pazar** **BULGARIA**
Dubrovnik Iskür _BALKAN MTS_
MONTE- **Pec** **Sofia** **Burgas**
Adriatic **NEGRO** **SERBIA**
Sea **Bar** L Shkoder △Musala **Plovdiv**
9590 **BYZANTINE EMPIRE**
Skopje **Adrianople**
Melnik RHODOPE MTS
Durazzo **Constantinople** **Nicomedia**
Ochrida Struma _Sea of_
Ohridsko L _Marmara_
Prespa L **Gallipoli** **Bursa**
Thessalonica _Thasos_ Sakarya
Vlore Aliakmon **GREECE**
Karies **OTTOMAN EMPIRE**
Mt Olympos _Lemnos_ ASIA MINOR
Corfu **Meteora** △9564
Corfu **Larisa** _Aegean_ _Lesbos_ **Phocaea**
Sea
PINDUS _Euboea_ _Chios_ **Volissos**
Ionian **Andinitsa** **Karistos**
_Is_ MTS
GREECE **ATHENS** _Andros_
Patras **Athens**
ACHAEA **Argos** _Naxos_ _Kos_
GREECE **Idra** **DUCHY OF**
Modon **Mistra** _Cerigo_ **NAXOS**
Rhodes
Rhodes

Crete **Candia**
Frangocastello

Black Sea

● Important settlement

Features located at a settlement
● Monastery
▲ Castle
■ University

△ 9564 Mountain peak (feet)
·—·—· Boundary, 14th century

Feet
6500
3250
650
0

Scale 1 : 8 000 000

0 _____ 200 km
0 _____ 150 miles

LITHUANIA, POLAND AND RUSSIA

The two most important states in the far eastern part of medieval Europe were Poland and Russia. In between these two great states stood Lithuania, which emerged as a separate state in the 13th century and by the end of the 14th century was combined with Poland under a Lithuanian king.

Poland

The name Poland comes from a Slavonic word, *pole*, meaning a field or plain. Its people were *poleni* – the inhabitants of the fields. Unlike in other areas of medieval Europe, here the territories controlled by tribes were joined together as a state quite early on in history. The first ruler was Mieszko I, who governed from 963 to 992. Soon after he took over he was converted to Christianity, and Poland became a Catholic state accepting the authority of the pope in Rome.

Mieszko established the Piast dynasty (ruling family) although he had to pay homage to the powerful German emperor. Poland did not survive long as one unified state. In the 12th century the land was ruled by a number of dukes but was reunited in the 14th century.

Russia

The land we know today as Russia developed in quite a different way. In the 10th century the cities around Kiev were linked together under the rule of descendants of merchant-soldiers who had come from Scandinavia. For a long time communities, whose wealth came from agriculture not trade, ruled themselves but they were overrun by the Mongol hordes from the Far East in the early 13th century. After this the Russians were divided into two main groups – the Great Russians and the White Russians. The Great Russians, whose power-base was the growing city of Moscow, emerged as the stronger group in the 13th and 14th centuries.

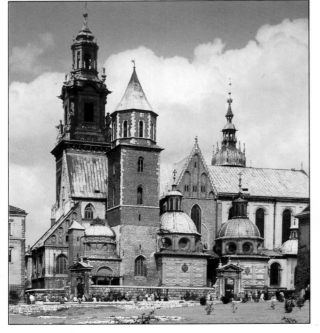

▽ Krakow in Poland was an important city in the development of the country. It became the headquarters (called the "seat") of the bishop in about 1000. The cathedral shown here was built in about 1018 but rebuilt in the 14th century. Krakow university was established in 1364.

△ Icons – images of God, Christ and the saints – were an important part of Russian Orthodox Christianity. This icon was made in the 14th century in Novgorod, Russia, and shows the Trinity with God as the father and the child Christ.

Important settlement

Features located at a settlement
- ● Monastery
- ■ University

—·— Boundary, 14th century

Feet
3250
650
0

Scale 1 : 9 000 000
0   200km
0   150 miles

Baltic Sea

Marienwalde
Poznan
Plock
Warthe
Wschowa
Lodz
POLAND
Radomsko
Krakow   Vist
Stary Sacz

A

Lake Onega

Kargopol

Velikii Ustyug

Lake Ladoga

Gulf of Finland

Neva

Staroladozhskii

Ferapontov

Sukhona

Oreshek

Blagoveschenskii

Volkhov

Vologda

Kirov

RUSSIA

Shcheremenskii

Novgorod

Borovich

Galich

Lovat

Krasnokholmskii

Unzha

Yaroslavl

Volga

Nikolaevskii Tikhonov

Kholm

Torzhok

Volga

Tver

Rostov

Gorodets

Nizhnii Novgorod

Suzdal

Volga

Braslav

Polotsk

Dvina

Moscow

Murom

Neman

Gzhatsk

CENTRAL

Vilna

Dnieper

Smolensk

Oka

RUSSIAN

Kaluga

Ryazan

Grodno

Minsk

UPLANDS

Novogrudok

Kirov

Don

Mogilev

Odoyev

ug

Wizna

Dankov

Warsaw

LITHUANIA

Pripet

Yelets

Warka

Brest

Turov

Lublin

Wlodximierz

Lutz

Chernigov

Desna

Lvov

Kiev

Halicz

Bjelgorod

Dniester

Bug

Poltava

Dnieper

B

C

D

4

3

2

1

A RUSSIAN VILLAGE

The scene below of a medieval village in Russia has been reconstructed from a number of different sources. Some buildings do survive, and there are drawings in manuscripts that also have written descriptions of village life.

Setting the scene

It was not until very recently that people living in towns and country villages could avoid the mud and slush caused by unpaved roads. Here it is winter, and in the houses the stoves (with no chimneys) provide the only warmth.

Buildings of wood

Russian villages and towns were built almost completely of wood – even Moscow, which became known as the Wooden City. Split tree trunks were laid to make the tracks usable. The houses were made of logs, and fire was the greatest hazard. Here, the chapel is also constructed from wood, even the roof. There was a great deal of very elaborate wood carving on some buildings, as on the little dome in our illustration. The cross standing on its own is also made of wood.

▷ In this scene, the boyar's weapons and the means of transport were inherited from the Mongols. The Mongols, as skilled warrior horsemen, overran northern China, north India and Russia as far west as the Black Sea. Their influence in Russia lasted until the end of the medieval period.

People and travel

It was obviously difficult to travel in such conditions. In Russia the sledge was very useful, especially over frozen ground and iced-over rivers. The central figure on horseback is a *boyar* – originally the title meant a leader of a tribe but it was later used for a nobleman who owned land. Between the chapel and the cross stands a bearded priest.

SCANDINAVIA

We have seen earlier (pages 24-25) how the early peoples – the Vikings – moved out from Scandinavia and invaded and settled far afield.

England and Scandinavia

In the 11th century under King Canute the histories of England and Scandinavia were connected. King Canute of England became king of Denmark in 1016 after his brother Harold died. He then moved into Norway in 1028. This military occupation was followed by Anglo-Saxon priests who converted people to Christianity and built churches.

By the 12th century Denmark had become a power in its own right and later conquered Norway and moved north along the coast of the Baltic Sea towards Finland.

Sweden

In the 13th century the Scandinavian peoples were not a unified group. In Sweden a number of great nobles ruled the country. Under one of them, Jarl Birger, in the mid-13th century, southern Finland was conquered.

Trading towns and the Baltic

The Vikings had established a number of trading posts, usually heavily fortified, in the Baltic. By the 12th century trade was in the hands of about 200 German towns which formed together into an association or league called the *Hanse* (the word meant a fellowship). Trading methods were made more efficient by bookkeeping and buying and selling on credit rather than exchange. The first center for the Hanse was at Wisby, but this was transferred to Lübeck, Germany, in the mid 13th century.

By the 15th century the power of the Hanse declined for three reasons. The Scandinavian countries joined together; the size of the herring shoals in the North Sea were declining; and trade was shifting to the Atlantic coasts.

Traded goods

Foreign agencies were established in England, France, Russia and Norway. Items of trade included fish, wine (from France and Germany), cattle (from Hungary and Poland), furs (from Russia), metals and wood (from Sweden), butter and cattle (from Denmark) and wool (from England).

△ Detail from a 12th-century tapestry in a church in Skog, a small town north of Stockholm, Sweden. The tapestry depicts the struggle between Christianity and paganism that took place at this time throughout much of Scandinavia.

◁ The testing of the sword – a detail of a 12th-century carving from a stave church portal illustrating the story of Sigurd, a hero of Norse mythology. The church is in Hylestad, about 160 mi southeast of Bergen, Norway.

5

Settements

■ Hanse town (see also pages 78–79)
● Important town

Features located at a settlement
● Monastery
▲ Castle

△ 6941 Mountain peak (feet)
–·–·– Boundary, 12th century (where known)

Feet	
	6500
	3250
	650
	0

Scale 1 : 7 500 000

0   200 km

0   150 miles

Lofoten Islands

Kebnekaise △ 6941

4

Torne

Lule

Kemi

L Imari

L Storaven

Ume

L Olujarvi

Norwegian Sea

Ströms Vattudal

● Trondheim

● Skog

3

FINLAND

L Saimaa

Gulf of Bothnia

NORWAY

Glittertind △ 8099

Sognefjorden
● Søgne

Glama

Ljusan

SWEDEN

L Nasijarvi

Lake Ladoga

● Bergen

Lagen

● Hamar

Klar

● Vyborg

● Turku

● Helsinki

● Oslo

● Stavanger

Skagerrak

● Hylestad

● Tonsberg

Gulf of Finland

● Vasteras

● Uppsala

L Malaren

● Birka ■ Stockholm ▲

L Vanern

● Skara

● Linkoping

Gotland

2

● Kungaly

L Vattern

■ Wisby ▲

● Alborg

● Varberg

● Viborg

DENMARK

● Vaxjo

● Kalmar ▲

Oland

● Aarhus ●

● Halsingborg

Baltic Sea

● Ribe ●

● Roskilde

● Copenhagen

● Malmö

● Svendborg

● Flensburg

● Trelleborg

● Schleswig ●

■ Kiel

A   B   C

1

Søgne, Norway

Although the first Christian king of Norway was Håkon "the Good" in the mid-10th century, there had been Christians in Scandinavia long before that. Archaeological evidence for Christianity comes from burials and stone monuments in the countryside. Churches must have been built by the missionaries in the 9th and 10th centuries, but no remains have been found so far. Any such churches were almost certainly built of wood.

Stave churches

Stave, that is wooden-planked, churches in Scandinavia were built to a simple plan. There was usually a rectangular nave and a square chancel with four central posts to hold up the roofs. Some of the churches had aisles. Outside, though, these churches were often very elaborate. Borgund church, shown here, has a series of roofs with complicated and detailed carvings of animals' heads.

▽ Borgund church, Søgne, in western Norway, was built in about 1150. The whole church, including the roof tiles, is built of wood. Between 1000 and 1300 all churches in Norway were wooden – about 700 in all. Today only 25 are still standing.

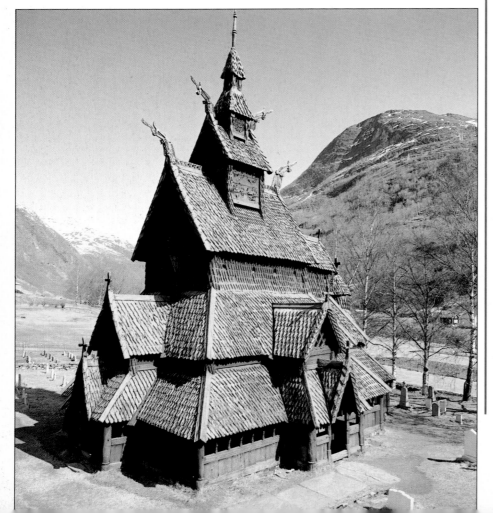

Trelleborg, Denmark

The site of Trelleborg in west Sjaelland is the best-preserved example we have of a Viking fortress. It was built and occupied between the middle of the 10th and the early 11th centuries, one of four very similar circular fortresses. These huge fortresses are unique in western Europe, although some people have suggested that the idea came from two of the Vikings' enemies – the Slavs (of central and eastern Europe) and the Saxons (of Germany).

Built to a careful plan

Like the other fortresses, Trelleborg must have been authorized by the king of Denmark. All four fortresses are built to a similar plan. They are round and divided inside into four regular quadrants, marked out by streets that cross the fortresses. The buildings, each of the same type, were set out inside the quadrants in fours around a courtyard. The layout of the fortresses and the buildings is based on a Roman measurement – the foot.

Solid defenses

Excavations at Trelleborg have shown that the defenses there are of earth with a wooden structure inside. Wooden palisades (fences) held this outer rampart together. At each of the four entrances there were large, heavy timber gates and guard towers. Beyond that was a ditch. Unlike the other fortresses, Trelleborg has another rampart running around it for extra protection.

Barracks and workshops

The buildings inside are all made of wood, with the roofs either thatched (as shown here) or covered in wooden tiles (called shingles). They are long, with the posts of the timber frames of the buildings set into the ground. These long buildings must have been barrack blocks for the troops.

Excavations also showed that there were a variety of small industrial workshops – such as for metalworking – on the site. It is possible that the taxes collected for the king were stored inside this heavily protected fortress.

▷ The fortress at Trelleborg differs from the other three in that it had an annex built (top right). The annex, which is protected by its own double rampart and ditches, contains thirteen more buildings of the same type as those inside the fortress.

▽ One corner of the fortress at Trelleborg shows the buildings in more detail. The rampart around the outside is built at two levels for strength and to allow access for guards. Each group of buildings may have had several uses — as barracks, as housing for local people in times of trouble or as centers of royal administration.

Søgne

Trelleborg

GLOSSARY

Aisle Part of a church, usually added at the sides of the nave, with its roof supported by columns.

Archaeologists People who work carefully, like detectives, to uncover the remains of the past, sometimes excavating for evidence, sometimes recording buildings or other structures.

Bailey The area of a castle, enclosed by an outer wall, in which the people lived.

Barbarians or barbari The word used by the Romans for any foreigner living beyond their boundaries who did not speak Latin.

Barrow A mound of earth heaped up over a burial.

Caliph The title of the ruler of Islam after the prophet Muhammad.

Canon A clerk who lived according to holy rules.

Castle A strongly fortified place built by the king or a local lord or ruler to protect their lands and to provide a safe place for themselves, their families and retainers.

Cathedral The main church of a bishop.

Chancel That part of the church where the priest conducts the service.

Chapter house The place in a monastery where the daily meetings of the religious community were held.

Cinque ports The name originally given to five ports on the south coast of England that were granted special privileges in return for certain duties.

Clinker-built boats Boats made from overlapping timber planks.

Condottieri Mercenary soldiers in 14th- and 15th-century Italy.

Crusade A religious war to win back the Holy Lands from non-Christians. The word comes from the habit of sewing crosses onto the soldiers clothing.

Diocese Term originally used for a district of the late Roman Empire. It is later used as a smaller district controlled by a bishop.

Domesday Book A record of property and its owners in England ordered by King William I in AD 1086.

Earthworks A term used by archaeologists to describe any remains (of earth) that can be seen on the surface of the ground.

East Roman Empire That part of the Roman Empire centered on the city of Constantinople (also known as Byzantium, now as Istanbul). Also called the Byzantine or Holy Christian Empire.

Empire A very large territory, usually covering more than one country, ruled by an emperor.

Fief Land granted by the king in return for military service.

Flying buttresses Supports of arches built on the outside of cathedrals to carry the enormous weight of the high roofs.

Fort or fortress The fortified place for a body of soldiers to live in.

Guild An association of merchants or craftsmen.

Hanse A trading association or league of German towns.

Hoards Collections of money or valuable goods that were buried or hidden in troubled times but never recovered by their owners.

Islam The religion of the Muslim peoples.

Keep The strongest part and last refuge of a castle. It is generally where the lord of the castle and his family lived.

Knight Originally meant an attendant. It came to mean a noble who served a king as a soldier on horseback who could provide arms and armor.

Manuscript A piece of writing made by hand and not printed.

Mercenaries Soldiers paid to fight.

Militia Local troops defending Italian towns until the 14th century.

Misericords or mercy seats Tip-up seats used by the clergy during long services.

Monastic Term used of a cathedral where the priests were monks.

Motte The mound, on which the keep usually stood, of the early timber and earth castles.

Muslim A believer in the Islamic religion.

Nave The part of a church where the congregation stand or sit for the service.

Orders Communities of monks or nuns who followed a Rule or code. There were also orders of knights established during the Crusades.

Parlement Originally the place for discussion in the French kingdom that became the chief royal court of law.

Parliament A group of adviser's established by the king in England to advise him. It has never lost the status of the highest court in the land.

Pilgrimage A journey (usually long) to visit the shrine of a saint. Pilgrims hoped their sins would be forgiven because they were making these journeys.

Shrine A holy place, perhaps where the remains of a saint are kept.

West Roman Empire That part of the Roman Empire centered on Rome (*see also* East Roman Empire). It eventually became broken up into the Frankish Empire and several barbarian states.

FURTHER READING

Reference books about the medieval period
How People Lived by Anne Millard (Silver Burdett) 1989.
A Viking Settler by Giovanni Caselli (Peter Bedrick Books) 1986.
A Medieval Monk by Giovanni Caselli (Peter Bedrick Books) 1986.
Cathedral: the Story of its Construction by David Macaulay (Houghton Mifflin) 1973.
The Observer's Book of Churches by L E Jones (Warne) 1969.
Castle by David Macaulay (Houghton Mifflin) 1977.
The Observer's Book of Castles by Brian Davison (Warne) 1979.
Life in a Medieval Village by Gwyneth Morgan (Lerner Publications) 1982.
Food and Cooking in Medieval Britain: History and Recipes by Maggie Black (English Heritage) 1985.
The Observer's Book of European Costume by G Squire & P Baynes (Warne) 1975.
Stories about medieval people
Dawn Wind by Rosemary Sutcliff (Puffin) 1982.
Dragon Slayer: The Story of Beowulf by Rosemary Sutcliff (Penguin) 1976.

The Dancing Bear by Peter Dickinson (Dell Publications) 1988.
The Road to Miklagard by Henry Treece (S.G. Phillips) 1957.
The Woolpack by Cynthia Hartnett (Methuen) 1951.
The Load of Unicorn by Cynthia Hartnett (Methuen) 1969.

Reference book for adults
Atlas of Medieval Europe by Donald Matthew (Facts On File) 1983.
The Oxford Illustrated History of Medieval Europe edited by George Holmes (Oxford University Press) 1988.
Past Worlds: The Times Atlas of Archaeology edited by Chris Scarre (Times Books) 1988.
The Archaeologist's Handbook by Jane McIntosh (Bell & Hyman) 1986.
Beowulf translated by David Wright (Penguin) 1957.
The Canterbury Tales by Geoffrey Chaucer translated by Nevill Coghill (Penguin) 1951.

GAZETTEER

The gazetteer lists places and features, such as islands or rivers, found on the maps. Each has a separate entry including a page and grid reference number. For example:

Alcala 73 C3

All features are shown in italic type. For example:

Andros, i. 83 B1

A letter after the feature describes the kind of feature:

i. island; *mt.* mountain; *mts.* mountains; *r.* river

Åarhus 89 B2
Aberdeen 67 C4
Abernethy 67 C4
Adrianople 83 B2
Agal 73 C2
Agen 55 C2
Agrigento 61 D1
Aisne, r. 55 C4
Aix 79 B2
Aix 79 B5
Ajaccio 61 B3
Akkerman 83 C3
Albarracin 73 D3
Albi 55 C1
Ålborg 89 B2
Alcacer do Sal 72 B2
Alcalá 73 C3
A lcalá de Guadaira 73 C1
Alcántara 72 B2
Alcázar de San Juan 73 C2
Alcobaça 72 A2
Algiers 8 C1
Alicante 73 D2
Allier, r. 8 C2, 55 C2
Almería 73 D1
Alnwick 67 C3
Alpirsbach 79 B4
Alps, mts. 9 C2, 61 B6, 79 B3
Alquézar 73 E4
Amboise 55 C3
Amiens 78 A4
Amsterdam 8 C3
Ancona 61 D4
Andinitsa 83 B1
Andros, i. 83 B1
Angers 55 B3
Angoulême 55 C2
Ankara 9 F2
Antwerp 79 A5
Aosta 61 B5, 79 B3
Apennines, mts. 9 D2, 61 D4, 79 C2
Appleby 67 C3
Ardfert 67 A2
Arezzo 61 C4
Argos 83 B1
Arlaniza 73 C4
Arles 79 A2
Armagh 67 B3
Armenis 83 B3
Arno, r. 61 C4, 79 C2
Arques 55 C4
Arras 55 C5
Arundel 67 C1
Ascoli 61 D4
Assaroe 67 A3
Asti 61 B5
Astorga 72 B4

Athens 9 E1, 83 B1
Athlone 67 B2
Auch 55 C1
Augsburg 79 C4
Aurillac 55 C2
Autun 55 D3
Auxerre 78 A4
Aviero 72 B3
Avila 73 C3
Axios, r. 9 C2
Ayr 67 B3

Badajoz 72 B2
Baeza 73 C2
Balearic Islands 8 C1, 73 E2
Balkan Mts 9 E2, 83 B2
Banff 67 C4
Baños de la Encina 73 C2
Bar 79 A2
Bar 83 B4
Barcelona 73 E3
Basle 79 B4
Bayonne 55 B1
Bazas 55 B2
Beaulieu 55 C3
Beaumaris 67 B2
Beaune 79 A3
Beauvais 55 C4
Bedford 67 C2
Beirut 9 F1
Beja 72 B2
Belém 72 A2
Belgrade 9 E2, 83 B2
Belluno 61 D5
Benevento 61 D3
Bere 67 B2
Bergen 89 A3
Berlin 9 D3
Berne 8 C2, 79 B3
Berwick 67 C3
Besalú 73 E4
Besançon 79 B3
Birka 89 B2
Bjelgorod 85 C2
Blagoveschenskii 85 C3
Blanc, Mont 8 C2, 61 B5, 79 B3
Bologna 61 C5
Bonn 8 C3
Bordeaux 55 B2
Borovich 85 C3
Boulogne 78 A5
Bourges 55 C3
Boyle 67 A2
Braganca 72 B3
Brandenburg 79 C5
Braslav 85 B3
Bratislava 83 A3
Bremen 79 B6
Brescia 61 C5
Breslau 79 D5, 83 A4
Brest 85 B2
Bridgnorth 67 C2
Brindisi 61 E3
Brive-la-Gaillarde 55 C2
Brixen 79 C3
Bruges 55 C5
Brünn 79 D4
Brussels 8 C3, 79 A5
Bucharest 9 E2, 83 B2
Buchau 79 B4
Budapest 9 D2
Budweis 79 C4, 83 A3
Bug, r. 85 B1
Burgas 83 B2
Burgos 73 C4
Bursa 83 B2
Bury St Edmunds 67 D2

Cadiz 72 B1

Caen 55 B4
Caernarvon 67 B2
Cagliari 61 C2
Cahors 55 C2
Calahorra 73 D4
Cambrai 79 A5
Cambrian Mts 67 C2
Cambridge 67 C2
Candia 83 B1
Cantabrian Mts 8 B2, 73 C4
Canterbury 67 D1
Capo d'Istria 61 D5
Carcassonne 55 C1
Carlisle 67 C3
Carpathian Mts 9 E2, 83 B3
Carrickfergus 67 B3
Cartagena 73 D1
Caspe 73 D3
Castel del Monte 61 E3
Castelo Branco 72 B2
Castillon 55 B2
Castledermot 67 B2
Catania 61 E1
Cattaro 61 F4
Celanova 72 B4
Cerigo, i. 83 B1
Châlons 55 D4
Channel Islands 8 B2
Charlieu 55 D3
Charroux 55 C3
Chartres 55 C4
Château Gaillard 55 C4
Chernigov 85 C2
Chester 67 C2
Chieti 61 D4
Chinchilla 73 D2
Chinon 55 C3
Chioggia 61 D5
Chios, i. 83 B1
Chur 79 B3
Citeaux 55 D3
Ciudad Real 73 C2
Ciudad Rodrigo 72 B3
Ciudadela 73 E2
Clairvaux 55 D4
Clermont-Ferrand 55 C2
Clitheroe 67 C2
Clonmel 67 B2
Cluj 83 B3
Cluny 55 D3
Coca 73 C3
Coimbra 72 B3
Colchester 67 D1
Cologne 79 B5
Como 61 C5, 79 B3
Compludo 72 B4
Constance 79 B4
Constantinople 83 B2
Conway 67 C2
Copenhagen 9 C3, 89 B2
Corbie 55 C4
Córdoba 73 C1
Corfe 67 C2
Corfu 83 A1
Corfu, i. 83 A1
Coria 72 B2
Cork 67 A1
Corsica, i. 9 C2, 61 C4
Corunna 72 B4
Cosenza 61 E2
Coutances 55 B4
Covadonga 73 C4
Crema 61 C5
Crete, i. 9 E1, 83 B1
Csanad 83 B3
Cuenca 73 D3

Dankov 85 C2
Danube, r. 9 E2, 79 D4, 83 B3
Dax 55 B1

Demirkazik, mt. 9 F1
Deventer 79 B5
Devizes 67 C1
Dijon 55 D3
Dinaric Alps, mts. 9 D2, 83 A2
Disentis 79 B3
Djakovo 83 A3
Dnieper, r. 9 F2, 85 C1
Dniester, r. 9 E2, 83 B3, 85 B1
Dolomites, mts. 9 D2, 79 C3
Don, r. 9 G2
Dordogne, r. 55 C2
Dortmund 79 B5
Dover 67 D1
Drava, r. 9 D2, 79 C3, 83 A3
Drina, r. 9 D2
Dubica 83 A3
Dublin 8 B3, 67 B2
Dubrovnik 83 A2
Dumio 72 B3
Dunaverty 67 C3
Dundalk 67 B2
Dunkeath 67 B4
Dunvegan 67 B4
Durazzo 83 A2
Durham 67 C3
Dvina, r. 9 E3, 85 C3
Dynevor 67 C1

Ebro, r. 8 B2, 73 C4
Edinburgh 67 C3
Eger 83 A4
Eger 83 B3
Eileen Donan 67 B4
Elbe, r. 9 D3, 79 C6, 83 A4
Erfurt 79 C5
Essen 79 B5
Esztergom 83 A3
Etampes 55 C4
Etna, Mount 9 D1, 61 D1
Euboea, i. 83 B1
Evora 72 B2
Exeter 67 C1

Fécamp 55 C4
Ferapontov 85 C4
Ferrara 61 C5
Fitero 73 D4
Flavigny 55 D3
Flensburg 89 A1
Fleury 55 C3
Florence 61 C4, 79 C2
Focsani 83 B3
Fontevrault 55 B3
Forfar 67 C4
Fossanova 61 D3
Frangocastello 83 B1
Frankfurt 79 B5
Frankfurt 79 C5
Fulda 79 B5

Galich 85 D3
Gallipoli 83 B2
Galway 67 A2
Garonne, r. 8 B2, 55 C2
Geneva 60 B6, 79 B3
Genoa 61 B5, 79 B2
Gerona 73 E3
Ghent 55 C5
Gibraltar 73 C1
Glastonbury 67 C1
Glogow 83 A4
Gloucester 67 C1
Gmünd 79 B4
Gorizia 79 C3
Gorodets 85 D3
Goslar 79 C5
Gotland, i. 9 D3, 89 B2
Granada 73 C1
Greifswald 79 C6

Grodno 85 B2
Groningen 79 B6
Guadalquivir, r. 8 B1, 73 C1
Guadalupe 73 C2
Guarda 72 B3
Gurk 79 C3
Gyulafehervar 83 B3
Gzhatsk 85 C3

Halicz 85 B1
Halsingborg 89 B2
Hamar 89 B3
Hamburg 79 C6
Hanover 79 B5
Hastings 67 D1
Havelberg 79 C6
Heidelburg 79 B4
Helsinki 9 E4, 89 C3
Hereford 67 C2
Herford 79 B5
Hermitage 67 C3
Holywood 67 B3
Huelgas 73 C4
Huelva 72 B1
Huesca 73 D4
Hylestad 89 A2
Hythe 67 D1

Iasi 83 B3
Idra 83 B1
Iglau 83 A3
Inch 67 B3
Ingolstadt 79 C4
Innsbruck 79 C3
Inverey 67 C4
Inverness 67 B4
Iona 67 B4
Ionian Islands 83 B1

Jaén 73 C1
Ják 83 A3
Jura Mts 8 C2, 79 B3

Kalmar 89 B2
Kalocsa 83 A3
Kaluga 85 C2
Kargopol 85 C4
Karies 83 B2
Karistos 83 B1
Kholm 85 C3
Kiel 79 C6, 89 B1
Kiev 85 C2
Kilia 83 B3
Kilkenny 67 B2
Killala 67 A3
Kirov 85 C2
Kirov 85 D3
Kizil Irmak, r. 9 F1
Klatovy 83 A3
Koblenz 79 B5
Königingrätz 79 D5, 83 A4
Kos, i. 83 B1
Krakow 84 A2
Krasnokholmskii 85 C3
Kungaly 89 B2

La Ferté 55 D3
La Couvertoirade 55 C1
La Rochelle 55 B3
Lamego 72 B3
Lancaster 67 C3
Langres 55 D3
Larisa 83 B2
Lausanne 79 B3
Le Mans 55 C3
Le Puy 55 C2
Leipzig 79 C5
Lelesz 83 B3
Lemnos, i. 83 B1
León 73 C4

Lérida 73 E3
Lesbos, i. 83 B1
Lescar 55 B1
Les Clairets 55 C4
Lesina 61 E3
Leyre 73 D4
Limerick 67 A2
Limoges 55 C2
Lincoln 67 C2
Lindau 79 B4
Linkoping 89 B2
Lisbon B1 8, 72 A2
Llandaff 67 C1
Loches 55 C3
Lodève 55 C1
Lodz 84 A2
Loire, r. 8 B2, 55 B3, 79 A3
London 8 C3, 67 D1
Londonderry 67 B3
Lot, r. 55 C2
Lourdes 55 B1
Louvain 79 A5
Luban 79 D5, 83 A4
Lübeck 79 C6
Lublin 85 B2
Lucca 61 C4
Lucera 61 E3
Luckau 83 A4
Lutsk 85 B2
Luxembourg 8 C2, 79 B4
Luxeuil 79 B4
Lvov 85 B1

Mâcon 79 A3
Madrid 8 B2, 73 C3
Majorca, i. 8 C1, 73 E2
Malaga 73 C1
Malmö 89 B2
Mantua 61 C5
Marburg 79 B5
Marienwalde 84 A2
Massif Central, mts. 8 C2, 55 C2
Medina del Campo 73 C3
Meissen 79 C5
Melnik 83 B2
Mende 55 C2
Menderes, r. 9 E1
Mérida 72 B2
Messina 61 E2
Meteora 83 B1
Metz 79 B4
Meuse, r. 8 C2, 79 B5
Milan 61 C5, 79 B3
Minorca, i. 73 E2
Minsk 85 B2
Miranda 72 B3
Mistra 83 B1
Modena 61 C5, 79 C2
Modon 83 B1
Mogilev 85 C2
Moissac 55 C2
Monaco 60 B4, 79 B2
Mondoñedo 72 B4
Monforte 72 B4
Montaner 55 C1
Montereau 55 C3
Montfort 55 C4
Montpellier 55 C1
Mt St Michel 55 B4
Montserrat 73 E3
Moscow 9 F3, 85 C3
Moulouya, r. 8 B1
Mulhacen, mt. 8 B1
Munich 79 C4
Münster 79 B4
Münster 79 B5
Murcia 73 D1
Murom 85 D3
Musala, mt. 9 E2, 83 B2

Nairn 67 C5
Nantes 55 B3
Naples 61 D3
Narbonne 55 C1
Naxos, i. 83 B1
Neman, r. 9 E3, 85 B3
Nevers 55 C3, 78 A3
Newcastle 67 C3
Newcastle-under-Lyme 67 C2
Nicomedia 83 C2
Nicopolis 83 B2
Nicosia 9 F1
Nikolaevskii Tikhonov 85 D3
Nîmes 55 D1
Nis 83 B2
Nitra 83 A3
Nizhnii Novgorod 85 D3
Nördlingen 79 C4
North Berwick 67 C4
Norwich 67 D2
Nottingham 67 C2
Novgorod 85 C3
Novi Pazar 83 B2
Novogrudok 85 B2

Ochrida 83 B2
Oder, r. 9 D3, 79 C6, 83 A4
Odoyev 85 C2
Ofen 83 A3
Oka, r. 9 G3
Oldenburg 79 B6
Olomouc 79 D4, 83 A3
Olympos, Mt 9 E2, 83 B2
Oporto 72 B3
Oradea 83 B3
Oreshek 85 C3
Orléans 55 C3
Orkney Islands 8 B3, 67 C5
Oslo 9 D3, 89 B2
Osma 73 C3
Otranto 61 F3
Oviedo 73 C4
Oxford 67 C1

Paderborn 79 B5
Paisley 67 B3
Palencia 73 C4
Palermo 61 D2
Palma 73 E2
Pamplona 73 D4
Paris 8 C2, 55 C4
Parma 61 C5
Passau 79 C4
Patras 83 B1
Pec 83 B2
Pécs 83 A3
Pembroke 67 B1
Peñafiel 73 C3
Périgueux 55 C2
Perth 67 C4
Perugia 61 D4
Peterborough 67 C2
Phocaea 83 B1
Piacenca 61 C5, 79 B3
Piedra 73 D3
Pierrefonds 55 C4
Pindus Mts 9 E1, 83 B1
Piombino 61 C4
Pisa 61 C4, 79 C2
Plasencia 72 B3
Plock 84 A2
Plovdiv 83 B2
Po, r. 9 D2, 61 C5, 79 B2
Poblet 73 E3
Poitiers 55 C3
Pola 61 D5
Policastro 61 E3
Polotsk 85 B3

Poltava 85 C1
Pontecorvo 61 D3
Pontigny 55 C3
Pontine Mts 9 F2
Porchester 67 C1
Portalegre 72 B2
Porto Torres 61 B3
Poznan 84 A2
Prague 9 D3, 79 C2, 83 A4
Premontré 55 C4
Pripet, r. 9 E3, 85 B2
Prut, r. 9 E2
Pyrennees, mts. 8 B2, 55 B1, 73 D4

Quedlinburg 79 C5
Quimper 55 A4

Rabat 8 B1
Raciborz 83 A4
Radomsko 84 A2
Ravenna 61 D5
Regensburg 79 C4
Reggio 61 E2
Reims 55 D4
Rennes 55 B4
Rethel 55 D4, 79 A4
Rhine, r. 9 C2, 79 B5
Rhodes 83 B1
Rhodes, i. 9 E1, 83 B1
Rhodope Mts 83 B2
Rhône, r. 8 C2, 61 A5, 79 B3
Ribas de Sil 72 B4
Ribe 89 A2
Richmond 67 C3
Rimini 61 D5
Ripoll 73 E4
Ritzebüttel 79 B6
Rochester 67 D1
Rodez 55 C2
Romney 67 D1
Roscommon 67 A2
Roskilde 89 B2
Rossano 61 E2
Rostock 79 C6
Rostov 85 C3
Rothenburg 79 C4
Rouen 55 C4
Roxburgh 67 C3
Royaumont 55 C4
Rutherglen 67 C3
Ryazan 85 C2

Sahagún 73 C4
Saharan Atlas, mts.8 C1
St Albans 67 C1
St Betrand 55 C1
St Brieuc 55 B4
St Clair 55 C4
St David's 67 B1
St Evroult 55 C4
St Maixent 55 B3
St Omer 55 C5
St Pol de Léon 55 B4
Salamanca 73 C3
Salerno 61 D3
Salisbury 67 C1
Saluzzo 61 B5
Salzburg 79 C4
Samos 72 B4
San Gimignano 61 C4
S Geronimo de Yuste 73 C3
San Juan de la Peña 73 D4
San Marino 9 D2
San Martin 73 E2
San Sebastian 73 D4
Sandwich 67 D1
Santa Creus 73 E3

Santafé 73 C1
Santander 73 C4
Santiago de Compostela 72 B4
Sao Vincente 72 B1
Saragossa 73 D3
Sarajevo 83 A2
Sardinia, i. 9 D2, 61 C3
Saros 83 B3
Sava, r. 79 D3, 83 A3
Scarborough 67 C3
Schleswig 89 A1
Schweinfurt 79 C5
Sées 55 C4
Segorbe 73 D2
Segovia 73 C3
Seine, r. 8 C2, 55 D4
Senj 83 A3
Sens 55 C4
Seville 72 B1
Shcheremenskii 85 B3
Shetland Islands 8 B4
Shrewsbury 67 C2
Sibenik 83 A2
Sicily, i. 9 D1, 61 D1
Siena 61 C4, 79 C2
Sierra Nevada, mts. 8 B1, 73 C1
Sierre 79 B3
Silistria 83 B2
Silves 72 B1
Siret 83 B3
Skara 89 B2
Skog 89 B3
Skopje 83 B2
Smolensk 85 C2
Sofia 9 E2, 83 B2
Søgne 89 A3
Soria 73 D3
Speyer 79 B4
Split 61 E4, 83 A2
Squillace 61 E2
Srebrenica 83 A2
Stablo 79 B5
Staroladozhskii 85 C4
Stary Sacz 84 B1
Stavanger 89 A2
Stettin 79 C6
Stirling 67 B4
Stockholm 9 D3, 89 B2
Strasbourg 79 B4
Ströms Vattudal 89 B3
Subiaco 61 D3
Sudenten Mts 74 D5, 83 A4
Suzdal 85 D3
Svendborg 89 B2
Syracuse 61 E1
Szatmar 83 B3

Tagus, r. 8 B1, 72 B2
Taranto 61 E3
Tarazona 73 D3
Tarbert 67 B3
Tarragona 73 E3
Tattershall 67 C2
Taurus Mts 9 F1
Thames, r. 67 C1
Thasos, i. 83 B2
Thessalonica 83 B2
Thouars 55 B3
Tiber, r. 9 D2, 61 D4
Tiranë 9 D2
Tisza, r. 9 E2
Toledo 73 C2
Tonsberg 89 B2
Toplerschlösschen im Rosenthal 79 C4
Tortosa 73 E3
Torzhok 85 C3
Toulouse 55 C1
Tournai 55 C5

Tours 55 C3
Transylvanian Alps, mts. 9 E2, 83 B3
Trelleborg 89 B1
Trent 79 C3
Treviso 61 D5
Trier 79 B4
Trifels 79 B4
Trim 67 B2
Trondheim 89 B3
Troyes 55 D4
Truro 67 B1
Tübingen 79 B4
Tumu Severin 83 B2
Tunis 9 D1
Turin 61 B5, 79 B3
Turku 89 C3
Turov 85 B2
Túy 72 B4
Tver 85 C3

Uppsala 89 B2
Utrecht 79 B5
Uzès 55 D2

Valencia 73 D2
Valladolid 73 C3
Vannes 55 B3
Varberg 89 B2
Varna 83 B2
Vasteras 89 B2
Vaxjo 89 B2
Velikii Ustyug 85 D4
Venice 61 D5
Ventadour 55 C2
Vercelli 61 B5
Vesuvius, Mount 61 D3
Vézelay 55 C3
Viborg 89 A2
Vicenza 61 C5, 79 C3
Vidin 83 B2
Vienna 9 D2, 79 D4
Villandraut 55 B2
Vilna 85 B2
Viseu 72 B3
Vistula, r. 9 D3, 84 B2
Viterbo 61 D4
Vlore 83 A2
Volga, r. 9 F3, 85 D3
Volissos 83 B1
Vologda 85 C3
Vosges Mts 79 B4
Vyborg 89 C3

Waidhofen 79 C4
Waldsassen 79 C5
Warka 85 B2
Warsaw 9 E3, 85 B2
Warwick 67 C2
Waterford 67 B2
Weser, r. 9 C3, 79 C5
Wigtown 67 B3
Winchester 67 C1
Windsor 67 C1
Wisby 89 B2
Wizna 85 B2
Wlodximierz 85 B2
Wschowa 84 A2
Würzburg 79 C4

Yaroslavl 85 C3
Yelets 85 C2
York 67 C2

Zadar 61 E5
Zagreb 83 A3
Zamora 73 C3
Zeitz 79 C5
Zilina 83 A3
Zurich 79 B3

INDEX

Page numbers in *italics* refer to illustrations or their captions.

Aachen 20
Abbot Suger 44
Africa, North *12*, 16, 17, 26, 72
Agilulf 17
Alaric 15
Alfred *25*
Alps 20
Angevin *see* Plantagenet
Angles 14, 15, *15*
animals 70, *70*
archaeological discoveries 22, 90
architecture 42-43, 63, 76, *82*
armies 16, 28, 30, 31, 68, 82
armor *17*, *22*, *31*
arts and crafts *10*, 14, *18*, *20*, 24, *38*, 46-47, *46*, *47*, 54, 63
assassination *54*
astrolabes *48*, 53
Athaulph 14
Attila the Hun 15
Augustus (Roman Emperor) 18
Augustus *see* Otto I
Austrasia 20

Baghdad, Siege of *82*
Baltic Sea 24
banking *65*
barbarians *12*, 14-15, 16, 17, 26
Basil I and II 26
battles 15, 16-17, *16*, *17*, 63;
    Hastings 28; 31, *33*
Bayeux Tapestry 30-31, *52*
Belisarius 16
Benedictine Rule 38
bibles *38*
birds *46*, *47*, 50, 70;
    see also falconry
Black Sea *87*
bleeding 48
Bohemia 37, 82
books *46*, 50, 52, *52*, 56, *70*;
    covers *10*, 15, *20*, *47*;
    production 49, 54;
    see also historians;
    histories; literature
boundaries:
    modern political *8-9*;
    territorial AD 350-1500 *12*, *13*, *15*, *16*, *17*, *26*, *55*, *61*, *67*, *72*, *73*, *83*, *85*, *89*
Bretwalda *see* Raedwald
bridges *52*, 58, *62*
British Museum 14, 22
bronze *20*, 22
building methods 38,

42-43, *66*, 68, 86, 90
Bulgars 17, 26, *26*
Burgundians 15, 20, 37, 54, 78, *78*
Burgundy 20, 37
burial customs 22-23, *24*
buried treasure *14*, 22-23
Byzantine Empire *13*, 17, 26-27, *26*, 48
Byzantium *see* Constantinople

campaigns
    of Charlemagne 20;
    of Henry I 37;
    of Justinian 16, 17;
    of Plantagenets 29;
    see also battles, Crusades
capital cities *8*, *9*, *26*, 72;
    see also settlements
Carolingian Empire 20-21
cartography 74-75
castles 28, *28*, 29, *29* 31, *34*, *35*, *37*, 66, *67*, 68-69, *78*, *79*, 80, *82*, *83*, *85*, 89
cathedrals 42-45;
    Chartres 43, 44-45;
    Krakow *84*; Lincoln 66;
    Notre-Dame, Paris *44*, 58; Santa Maria del Fiore, Florence 63
Catholic church 66, 84
chain mail *31*
Charlemagne (Charles the Great) *12*, 20-21, *20*, 28
Chartres cathedral 43, 44-45
Chaucer, Geoffrey 52
children 35, 40, *65*
China *87*
Christianity *12*, *13*, 22, *26*, 34-35, 38-39, 44-45, 72, 76, 84, *84*, 88, 90
    in England *10*; in France 15; in Ireland *66*; in Italy 18; in Rome 26; in Spain 72
Churches 18, *20*, *31*, 38 *38*, *39*, 63, 76, *80*, *82*, 90, *90*
    Conques *76*; Sacra Croce, Florence, 18, St Sophia, Istanbul *27*; San Vitale, Ravenna 16 *18*, *18*; Santillana, Spain *76*
    see also cathedrals;
    stave churches
Cinque ports 66, *67*
city walls 58, 60, 62 *63*, 72
    see also fortified cities
clocks 80
cloth 62, *64*, 65, 81
Clovis 20, 58
Cluny 38
compasses 53
Compostela 56, 76-77

condottieri 60
Conrad of Franconia 36
Constantine the Great 26
Constantinople *12*, *13*, 17, 18, *22*, 24, 26, *27*, 63, 82
cooking 81
cotton *64*
crossbows 35
crosses *20*, *38*, *66*, 86
crowns 15
Crusades *13*, 34-35, *34*, 54, 63, 64, *82*
Czechs 82

Danelaw *25*
Danes 28, 68
Dante Alighieri 63
Denmark 88
Diocletian *12*, *13*
Domesday Book 32-33
dyes 63

East Anglia 24
East Roman Empire
    see Byzantine Empire;
    Roman Empire
education 40-41
    see also universities
Edward the Confessor 28, 30, *30*, 33, 66
Emperors *see* Roman Emperors
empires *see* Carolingian;
    Frankish; Holy Roman
    Empire; Justinian;
    Plantagenet; Roman
enamel *20*
entertainment 47, *49*, 52
European Community (EC) 8
everyday life 70, *70*, 80, 86-87

fairs *64*, 65
falconry *50*, *70*
farm buildings *25*
farming 33, *33*, *54*, 62, 70, *70*
Flanders 78
Florence 62-63
food *64*, 65, 70, *81*, 88
fortified cities and towns *16*, *17*, *35*, *36*, *37*, 56, *56*, *57*, 62, *62*, 68, 73, 90
Frankish Empire *12*, *13*
Franks *12*, *13*, 15, *15*, 20, 52
Frederick of Germany 35
furs 24, 88
fustian *64*

Gaul 14, 20
Genghis Khan *87*
Genoa 63, 65
Geoffrey of Anjou 28
German Empire *see* Holy Roman Empire
glass 44

stained 44-45
gold (metal) 26, *64*
gold (objects) 14, *20*
Gothic style 42-43
Goths 14, 15, 18
    government 81
    in England 66; in France 54-55, 68; in Germany 78; in Italy 60-61, 62, 63; in the Low Countries 78; in Switzerland 78; in Wales 66
grain *64*, 65
Greece 82
Greek classics 63
Greeks 18, 74
guilds 62, *65*, 81
Gutenberg, Johann 49

Hanse (Hanseatic League) 88
Hapsburgs 78
Harald of Norway 30
Harold (Norman King) 28, 30, *30*, 31, *31*
heathens 24
helmets 20, 31
Henry I of Saxony 36, 37
Henry II of England 28, *28*, *29*
Henry the Navigator 75
historians:
    Ammianus Marcellinus 14; Bishop of Freising *57*; Froissart 58; Ordericus of Vitalis 40; Procopius 14
histories 32
    Anglo-Saxon Chronicle 24, *32*; Book of Marvels *52*
    see also Bayeux Tapestry, Domesday Book
Holy Land 13, 34, 72
Holy Roman Empire *13*, 36-37, *37*, 78, *78*, 82
honey 24
houses 25, *66*, *91*
Hülegü *87*
Hungary 82
Huns 15, *15*, 17
hunting *28*, 56, 70, *70*

icons *84*
illness 48, *49*
illuminated manuscripts *10*
India *87*
industries 80, 81
    see also cloth, pottery, wool
Ireland 66
Islam *12*, *13*, 26, 72
ivory *10*, *47*

jewelry 15, *18*
Justinian 14, 16-17, *16*, *17*, 18, 26, *26*
Jutes 14, 15, *15*

Khusrau I 17
kings
    Anglo-Saxon *25*;
    Bohemian 82;
    Carolingian 20; Danish 88; East Anglian 22;
    English 28, 29, 30, 35, 88; Frankish 20, 58;
    French 35, 54-55;
    German 16, 35, 36-37;
    Lombard 17; Norwegian 30; Ostrogoth 15, 16, 18; Polish 84; Spanish 35, 60
knights *34*, 35
    St John the Hospitalers *35*, *56*, 82; Templars *35*, *56*; Teutonic *35*, 37

Lanfranc 40
languages 20, 36, 49
law (teaching of) 40, 63
leather *22*, *64*
leeches 48
Leonardo da Vinci 48, *48*
Lindau Gospels *20*
Lindisfarne *10*, 24
Lindisfarne Gospels *10*
linen *30*, *64*
literature 46-47, *50*, 52, 63
    classics 20
Lithuania 84
Lombards 17, *17*, *37*, 60
longships 24, 31, 52
Louis IX 35, *44*, 54
Luxembourgs 78
lyre *22*

Macedonians 26
Magyars 36, 37
Manuel I 26
manuscripts 20, 37, 40, 41, *47*, 54
maps 53, 74-75
markets *see* fairs
Martel, Charles 20
mathematics 74
Matilda 28
Maximian *12*
Medici family 60, 63
medicine 40, 48, *49*, 63
Mediterranean Sea 64
mercenaries 14, 60
metalwork *14*, 15, 37, 64
Middle East 26
Mieszko I 84
monasteries 20, 38, *41* 52, *54*, *55*, *67*, 72, *73* 77, *78*, *79*, *83*, *85*, *89*
monastic life 38, 47
money changing 65
Mongols 82, 84, *87*
monks 38, *40*, 42, 44
mosaics 16, 18
mosques 27
mother-of-pearl *18*
motte-and-bailey *see* castles

mountain ranges 8, *8*, *9*
music 40, 47, *47*, 52
Muslims 12, *13*, 17, 20, 26, 34, *35*, 48, 54, 72, 76, 82

Narbonne 15
Narses 16
nation states *13*
navigation 48, 74
Neustria 20
Normans 28, 30-31, 42-43, 66, *66*, 69
North America 24, *24*, *25*
nuns 38

Odo of Bayeux *30*, *31*, 33
Ordovacar 16
Ostrogoths 14, 15, *15*, 17, 18, 20
Otto I 36, 37
Ottoman Turks *13*, 17 26, 82

pack animals 65
pagan burial 22
paganism 88
Paris 58-59
parliament 54, 66
pattern books 46
peoples *13*, *15*, *16*, *17*, *37*
Pepin III 20
perfumes 63
Persians 17
Philip II of France 35
philosophy 40
pilgrimages 34-35, 52, *56*, 64, 76-77, *77*
Piracy 64
place names 66
plainchant (plainsong) 47
Plantagenet Empire 28, 29
playing cards *49*
plowing *33*, *70*
Poland 84
Pomerania, Duchy of 37
Pompeii *18*
popes 20, 38
    Gregory I (the Great) *10*,
    47 Gregory VII *37* Leo III
    20, 26 Urban II 34
populations *66*, 80
    Roman Empire *12*
Portugal 26, 72, *74*, *75*
pottery 80
precious stones 63
printing 49, *49*, 74
Procopius 14
Prussia 37

Raedwald 22
Ravenna 15, 16, 18-19
religion *see* Christianity, Islam
religious objects 34
Richard I 35
roads 52, 66
Roman army 16
Roman Britain 14

Roman emperors *12*, *13*,15, 16-17, 18
Roman Empire *12*, *13*, 15, 16-17, 26, 38, 48, 60
    see also Byzantine Empire
Roman navy 18
Romanesque style *76*
Romans 8, 12, 14, 15 72
Rome 16, 34, *60*
rose window 43, *44*
Russia 84, 87

saints 76
Saladin 35
Saracen Turks 20
Saxons 14, 15, *15*, 20, 28, *33*, *66*, 68
Scandinavia 88
science *47*, 48
sculpture 46
sea charts 74
seafaring 24
Seljuks 26
settlements, major
    AD350-1500
    12, *13*, *16*, *17*, *24*, *25*, *29*
    35, *61*, *67*, *72*, *73*, *78*, *79*
    83, *85*, *89*
sheep 25
shields 22
shipbuilding *24*, *31*
ships *22*, *23*, *24*, 31, *52*, 65
sieges 16, *35*, 87
Silesia, Duchy of 37
silk *64*
silver (metal) 24
silver (objects) *14*, *22*
slaves 23, 33, 35
Slavs *13*, 17, 36, 37
Spain 26, 72-73, *76*
spears *22*, 35
spices *62*, 63, *64*
spinning wheels 80
stained glass 44-45, *81*
statues *20*, *27*
stave churches 90, *90*
Stephen 28, 29, *29*
stonemasons 42, *42*, 46, 63
Suevi *15*
sugar 64
Sutton Hoo 22-23
Sweden 88
Switzerland 78
swords *22*
Syria 26

taxes 52, 66, 90
teaching 40-41
    see also law, universities
technology 48-49
    see also building methods
Templar Knights *35*, *56*
tesserae 18
Teutonic Knights *35*, 37
textiles 64-65, *64*

Theodora 18, *18*
Theodoric 15, 16, *16*, 18
Theodosius *12*, 15, 26, 38
Thetford treasure *14*
timber 24, *64*, 65, 86
towns *see* fortified towns, houses, villages
trade 16, 24, *58*, 62, 63, 64-65, *81*, 88
trades *37*, 65
    see also cloth; industries
transport 52-53, 65, 86
travel 52-53
    see also ships; trade
Trelleborg *91*
troubadours 47

universities 40, 54, *54*, *55*, *78*, *79*, *83*, *84*, *85*, *89*

Vandals 15, *15*, 16, 26
Vatican 20
Venetian ports 65, *68*
Venice 60, 63
Vikings 24-25
villages 86-87
    see also everyday life
Viscontis 60
Visigoths 14, 15, *15*, 20
volcanic eruption *25*

Wales 66
warships 24, 31, *33*
water mills 80
weapons *22*, 31, *31*, 35
West Roman Empire *see* Roman Empire
William the Conqueror 30-33, *31*, *52*
windmills 80
wine *64*, 88
women 65, *81*
wood carvers *46*, *80*, 86, 90
wool industry 64, *64*, 88
Worms 15

York *66*